M000227926

Also by The Financial Diet

The Financial Diet: A Total Beginner's Guide to Getting Good with Money

BEYOND GETTING BY

BEYOND GETTING BY

The Financial Diet's Guide to Abundant and Intentional Living

Written by Holly Trantham
Designed by Lauren Ver Hage
Foreword by Chelsea Fagan

Crown Currency
New York

Copyright © 2024 by TF Diet LLC

All rights reserved.

Published in the United States by Crown Currency,
an imprint of the Crown Publishing Group,
a division of Penguin Random House LLC, New York.

CROWN is a registered trademark and CROWN CURRENCY
and colophon are trademarks of Penguin Random House LLC.

Hardback ISBN 978-0-593-72796-6
Ebook ISBN 978-0-593-72797-3

Printed in China on acid-free paper

crownpublishing.com

987654321

First Edition

Book design by Lauren Ver Hage

Illustrations by Cindy Niu | www.cindyniu.com

To Peter, whom building a life with could simply not be better

To Joe and Lily (and our sweet baby on the way!), who make every day feel like magic

And to anyone who has found in TFD a refuge to talk about money free from shame, judgment, or expectation

CONTENTS

AUTHOR'S NOTE

This book is intended solely as a source of inspiration and information for readers who wish to move beyond the getting-by phase of their financial lives. Examples of typical financial situations and solutions to common problems are included for illustrative purposes only. If the reader needs advice concerning the evaluation and management of specific legal or financial risks or liabilities, such as bankruptcy or tax matters, they should seek the help of a licensed, knowledgeable professional.

FOREWORD

THE DEATH OF THE GIRLBOSS AND THE RISE OF THE GIRLLOCAL-UNION-DELEGATE

By Chelsea Fagan,

Founder and CEO of The Financial Diet

Dearly beloved, we are gathered here today in our business casual best to mourn the untimely and unfortunate death of the girlboss.

She came in many forms, and she struggled valiantly against the rising wave of exhaustion at her particular brand of pinkwashed-capitalism-as-liberation, but I think it's fair to say that we can finally put her to rest.

As we gently lower her tasteful mid-century modern casket, well funded as it was by increasingly frantic rounds of venture capital and sponsored in partnership with Smartwater and Peloton, we can only hope that her demise will seed a brighter, more verdant, and more class-conscious vision of what it means for a woman to be liberated.

The individual girlbosses themselves may have mostly met professional fates of scandal, HR meltdowns, bankruptcy, and discrimination lawsuits, but the countless women who worked underneath them while they were splashed across the pages of *Forbes* and *The Wall Street Journal* still have much to contribute. The role women should play at home and in the workplace is still a question largely left unanswered, and the girlboss only derailed us another decade or so in the wrong direction.

Put simply, the idea that a rich (and usually white) woman's success anywhere is a victory for women everywhere, or that an executive board that contains a token woman balances out a company where women don't have maternity leave, is utter bullshit. And while the revolution to put women in the workplace was a resounding success—to the extent now that most of us don't have a choice in the matter, even when we're also full-time mothers—there was no such revolution to bring men into the home. There was no such revolution to use an effectively doubled workforce to reduce the overall hours we have to work. In fact, our wages have only stagnated or decreased in that time, regardless of gender, with inflation far outpacing wage growth since the late sixties. And the girlboss temporarily convinced us that as long as we looked chic enough doing it, giving over our identities and the majority of our waking hours to our employers and to the relentless pursuit of individual wealth could be considered power.

In the six years since I wrote *The Financial Diet: A Total Beginner's Guide to Getting Good with Money*, I have become certain that this is a lie, even if you are the CEO of the company in question. I am, in fact, a CEO, and my company—also called The Financial Diet—has grown substantially since I wrote that book. My co-founder (and designer of both this book and that one) has become a mother, as have other women on our team. That team has weathered a pandemic, we've gotten married, we've held conferences over Zoom, we've taken PPP loans, and we've remained both nimble and lucky enough to still be here, personally and professionally. But none of us, not even in our toughest moments, has given in to the superficial allure of hustle culture.

We have shifted to a four-day workweek and never looked back (and I'll be back later in this book to talk about that), and we have reduced the hours we work and the extent to which we rely on that work for our identities. We've expanded our benefits, strengthened our maternity leave, increased our salaries, and done everything as a company with a singular

focus: helping ourselves and those we reach to live a better life financially, without ever making money the goal in and of itself.

Because yes, money is essential to life (at least for now, comrades), and managing it well is often the difference between freedom and constraint, options and coercion. But once you have enough of it, the focus should be on converting that money into things that are actually meaningful to you: more time with the people you love, more creativity, more days to just vibe on the couch and watch a whole season of a mid-tier Netflix show if you so choose. Rather than constantly pushing yourself toward the next promotion or bonus, how can you help someone a little earlier in their career to get theirs? Instead of constantly fretting over saving every possible penny, how can you live abundantly and generously with the people around you, in both financial and emotional terms? Now that you've got a hold on your basic finances, what role does money actually serve in your life? And unlike the recently deceased girlboss, how are you going to form an identity that isn't about monetizing or optimizing every waking second of that life?

If the first TFD book was a primer in getting your head above water financially and understanding the basics of building freedom and security—and if you haven't read it yet, I suggest you do—this book is all about what comes next. As the title indicates, it's about going beyond just getting by in your life, not only in terms of money, but also in terms of how you view yourself, how you value your time, and how you form communities with the people around you. If you succeed at the

The first TFD book!

expense of everyone else, that isn't a victory. If you raise a ton of venture capital and pay your employees like shit, you're not a feminist icon. And if you have accumulated a bunch of money but have no time to actually live the life that money was supposed to be for, congratulations, you've played yourself.

And because I try to live my values (or, at least, my personal catchphrases), I am passing the torch of writing the majority of this very book to my longtime colleague and collaborator Holly Trantham. She has worked for The Financial Diet nearly as long as I have, touches almost every piece of editorial we produce, and has in many ways defined the ethos of our brand alongside me. She's also, as it happens, a woman who is excellent with money and has a keen understanding of how to explain more-complicated financial concepts in ways that are digestible and easy to understand. She is the perfect person to write this book, and she will be your shepherd as you progress to the next level on every topic we cover at TFD. (Don't worry, though, my talkative ass will be popping in on topics I simply *have* to give my thoughts on.)

So before we dive in, let me leave you with this: If the girlboss is dead, let her rest in peace, and give her her flowers for what she was able to accomplish in her time. She built some massive companies (most of which are now gone, but still), she pulled off some truly epic scams (and is likely to serve only *some* jail time), and she gatekept and gaslit all the way to the top of every 30-Under-30 list. She gave us the ethos of "We can do anything a man can do," to which we can now confidently say, "Yeah, but what men do absolutely sucks, and we don't want to do any of that," and move on to something totally new and better, regardless of gender. Work is not the point of life, and neither is money. So let's stop trying to get ahead, and start trying to go beyond getting by.

BEY
GET

OND
TING
BY

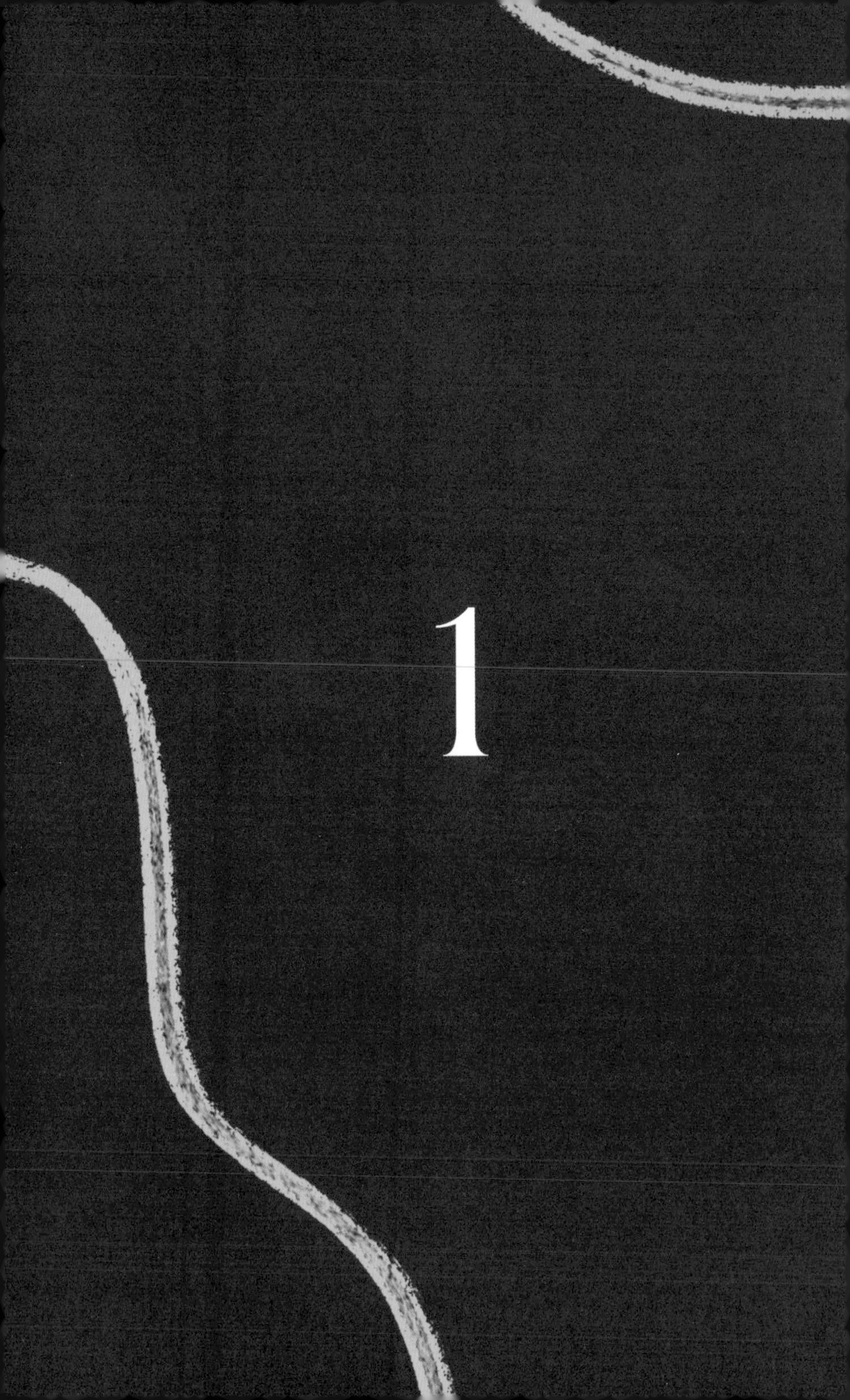

1

MOVING BEYOND GETTING BY IS A PRACTICE, NOT A CHALLENGE

In May of 2016, I took a web editor job I found on Craigslist. I know you must be thinking, *Girl, I could have told you not to do that.* But bear with me.

I was twenty-four, barely scraping by after years of temp work, unpaid media internships, short stints in corporate "real jobs," and various freelance writing and editing gigs. I was sick of not knowing how much I was going to make in a given month and having to hunt down paychecks from the crappy entertainment news websites and SEO factories I was working for. I wanted so badly to find my dream job, doing creatively fulfilling writing and editing, but I also just wanted to know when my next check was coming. And I wanted to take a nap.

Finding that job listing felt like fate. The company was an early-phase, membership-based start-up that would be putting on events with local artists. It was an actual full-time position, not just a contractor role operating on a "we'll pay you when we feel like it" timeline. The work I would be doing sounded genuinely compelling: interviewing artists for the website to drive interest in the membership program. Best of all, it was self-funded by the founder—my boss, who had previously worked on Wall Street—who explained how great it was that we wouldn't be beholden to the expectations of outside investors.

As with any start-up lacking a clear business plan, the situation was inevitably too good to be true. After getting paid for precisely one week of work (in cash, because he was having "bank issues" and wouldn't be able to get me a check for a while), I never saw a cent that the company owed me. Yet I stuck around for two more months, for a few reasons. My boss was exceptionally

Unpaid Internship (n.): a company's excuse to squeeze free labor out of eager college students and twenty-somethings under the guise of "experience," while gatekeeping opportunities for those who can't afford to work for free

charismatic and personable. He bought us lunch every single day! How could someone who always treats you to lunch, *including* a one o'clock beer, possibly be scamming you?

Plus, when I asked more questions about the status of my paycheck while apologizing for being pushy, he insisted I should never be sorry for insisting on getting paid what I was owed. He made me truly believe he cared about me, and he seemed to go out of his way to show me that the delays were genuine. He once even took me to a legit brick-and-mortar bank to meet with his banker, who basically reiterated the same reasons why my pay was being delayed (reasons that were likely made up but sounded way over my head). Looking back, I can see that he used that feeling of connection to manipulate me into staying, even when I'd gone weeks, then months, without seeing a paycheck.

I was also stubborn. I quickly emptied the meager emergency fund I'd managed to save up in the months prior to finding that fated job ad, and I landed myself back in credit card debt to cover my bills. I'd update my mom on the situation almost every day, trying to downplay her anxiety and reiterate that my boss was a good guy who wouldn't just *not pay me*. I'd insist to my then-boyfriend, now-husband, Peter, that everything would turn out fine—that I'd eventually be paid and life would return to normal. But even *I* didn't believe what I was telling them, and deep down, I just didn't want to admit that I'd made a colossal mistake. And as I was digging myself deeper and deeper into a financial hole, I'd already given so much of my time to this "company." If I left, there was a better possibility that I'd *never* see what I was owed.

But there was something else going on. Up until that point in my career, I'd taken part-time and freelance editor contracts, and I had worked as a blog editor at a women's magazine, but I'd never been offered a full-time, salaried position with "editor" in the title. I didn't really believe I was experienced enough to get the job in the first place, even though I'd been editing in various capacities for years. I'd never worked for a mainstream media outlet, so why was I being trusted with the content of a totally new website? So, even when I went day after day not being paid, I didn't feel like my own time was valuable enough to cut my losses and leave.

Now, years later, I can look back and laugh about how naive I was. I left after finding out that another young woman, who had been at the company when I joined and was let go just a few weeks into my tenure, also didn't see a paycheck after her first one. It finally clicked that staying wasn't the answer, and that the longer I spent working toward nothing, the more time I would lose trying to get work that, you know, actually paid me. Thankfully, it was just a blip in my financial growth; after getting paying work again, I slowly built back my emergency savings. And luckily, I had good credit thanks to parents who encouraged me to open my first credit card and start building a credit history in college. If you've read the first TFD book, you know that good credit means you simply have more options; I quickly got approved for a new balance-transfer credit card with a 0% APR period for fifteen months, which allowed me to pay off the (admittedly small) debt I accrued without paying exorbitant interest.

I still have no idea what my former boss was up to—I've never gotten any answers on why I wasn't paid, or what that "business" must have been a front for. And yes, those unanswered questions occasionally keep me up at night. But I mostly feel awful for the person I was then, who didn't value herself enough to see when she was clearly being manipulated. I wanted to be paid what I was owed, yes, but I also thought I owed my boss (a total stranger whom I *to this day* can't find on the internet) my time, simply because he offered me a job when I was feeling down on myself. I hadn't yet learned when to walk away.

Needless to say, starting my job at The Financial Diet in the fall of 2016 was quite a boon for me. I had been checking the blog daily, seeking solace as I was getting back on my feet after such a huge-seeming setback, when I came across the job listing for a new managing editor. I shot my shot, and it worked out—I've been here ever since.

In those early days at TFD, I'd assign, edit, and write articles on every possible money topic, from the difference between a Roth and traditional

IRA to the cost of a heart-shattering breakup. I was part-time for those first few years, making as much as the company could afford to pay me (which was. . . . still quite a bit more than many NYC media companies seem to pay). I've since moved up to my current position as creative director, where we still talk about money, though the context and format have evolved.

We've shifted away from the blog and now publish to an audience of millions across YouTube, podcasting, social media, and our semiweekly newsletter. We have an entire events department that didn't even exist when I joined, but that now makes up a significant portion of our revenue. Our staff has more than doubled in size. And instead of just covering the basics of getting your money right (although we'll always do that!), our content ranges from dismantling the myths that capitalism has implanted into our brains to what our cultural obsession with "TikTok face" is costing us.

Back in 2016, our core audience was (mostly) women in the same spot I had been in: fumbling their way through the professional world and starting out on their journeys with money. As our readers and viewers were learning about investing in retirement and opening their own accounts for the first time, I was right there with them, figuring out how to save and invest and still have enough left over to buy overpriced pastries and visit my beloved Broadway sing-along bar every month.

By certain metrics, my financial life remains unimpressive: I don't own a home and, considering I live in New York City with no desire to move, don't know if I ever will. I've stuck it out with one company for a long time instead of job-hopping to maximize my earning

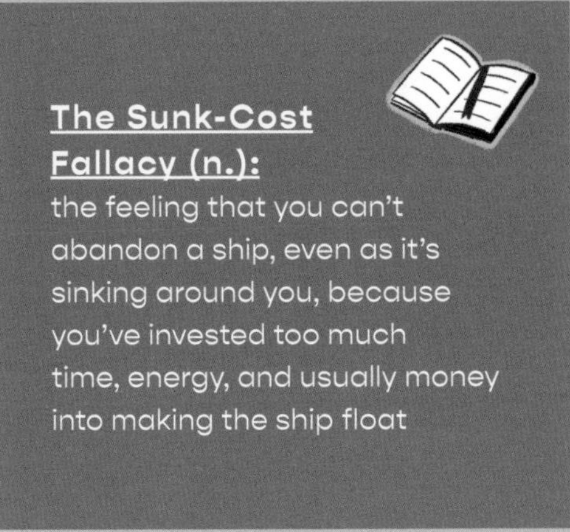

potential. I haven't invested in an Airbnb empire or raised millions in venture capital for a start-up. And the amount of money I spend on dining out each month would make the FIRE bros of the world nauseous with anxiety. I'm not a millionaire, let alone a billionaire.

But by most metrics, I'm quite financially successful. I earn well over the average household income for the U.S., even excluding my husband's income. I'm able to max out my yearly 401(k) contributions.

I have paid off all my debt, live in a totally debt-free household now that we've finished paying off my husband's student loans, and am investing in other long-term goals besides retirement.

I can confidently say I'm good with money. I'm taking care of my financial future, and I don't have to sacrifice things I genuinely want. I've learned to differentiate between my own values and what I've simply been taught should be important to me. And most of all, I know the value of my money, but also my time. Yes, I have a job that fulfills me and provides me with a more-than-livable wage, but it also doesn't play an outsize role in my life. It gives me enough free time to pursue my many other interests. I'm sure that, at this point in my career, I could move on to something that technically gives me a bigger salary, but at what cost? Giving my energy to a big corporation that doesn't care about me, all so I can have less free time and flexibility than I do now? Being proud of the work I do while also having the time to build a fulfilling life beyond work: That is the biggest luxury I can think of.

Throughout my early-career days, I couldn't have pictured myself writing about personal finance, because money wasn't something I ever really thought about, other than when I had an absence of it. I wouldn't have imagined myself producing YouTube videos and podcast episodes, either, because I didn't realize I had a skill set that would lend itself to that kind of job. My career has evolved more than I could have imagined—but so has my relationship with work itself. And I owe that, in part, to having this job that requires me to examine the systems we live in. By necessity, I'm constantly thinking about what actually makes us happy and, by extension, what actually makes *me* happy. Because the truth is—in the same way I told myself I didn't deserve to be paid for my work—we've *all* been sold lies about wealth, work, and security that are actively making our lives worse.

For nearly a decade now, my work life has been dedicated to identifying these lies so that we can all live better, more fulfilling lives. As conscientious, independently minded women, our adult lives are already filled with contradictions. We want to live well while also working to improve quality of life on a systemic level. We want to do work that fulfills us and pays us what we're worth without sacrificing every waking hour to the grind. We want to be fully present for our loved ones without being reduced exclusively to our roles as wives or daughters or mothers. My aim with this book is to address how we can make sense of these contradictions to better inform how we actually want to live.

Throughout this book, I'll be discussing two main themes that, over my years working at TFD, I've determined are most valuable when it comes to living a more fulfilling, happier life: ***abundance*** and ***intention***.

When you think of abundance, you may be actually thinking of excess—always acquiring more and trying to level up, without questioning why. In our era of massive signing bonuses for soul-crushing jobs and endless fast-fashion-haul videos on our social media accounts, we're fed the message that *more* is synonymous with *better*. But living abundantly really means knowing that there is enough to go around, so periods of acquisition and periods of restraint will naturally ebb and flow. When you don't personally have enough, abundance means understanding that you deserve more, and that you shouldn't feel ashamed to go after it. And when you *do* have enough, abundance means knowing when it's time to pay it forward, or when having more time is more important than having more money.

Living with intention, therefore, doesn't contradict an abundance mindset; rather, it works in conjunction with it. The more intentional you are about your money, the more it can help facilitate the life you want. This can mean weighing your spending decisions beforehand to make the best long-term choices. Is this going to be something that brings you value for years to come? Could it potentially contribute to a cherished memory? Will you have to sacrifice any other financial aims to cover the cost? Intention can also mean assessing your income goals from multiple angles, not simply "pick the one that's going to make me the most money." Does the company you're interviewing with share your value system? Is this additional freelance client worth the free time you'll have to sacrifice to work on the project? Are there nonfinancial benefits to sticking with your less-than-dreamy day job?

When I compare my life now to the struggle bus I was riding before finding TFD, I can't believe how lucky I've been. If I could have looked three, four, five years into the future and seen what I had coming, I would have left that sketchy start-up without a second thought. But I also know that just because I'm lucky doesn't mean I don't deserve what I have gotten, because we *all* deserve to live lives that fulfill us. Hopefully, you won't land yourself in a Craigslist job scam. But that doesn't mean you won't find yourself stuck in a too-demanding career you're afraid to leave, or living a restrictively frugal lifestyle you feel you can't abandon, simply because of the time you've sunk into it. You are always allowed to change course. And there is more than enough to go around, especially once you really define what "enough" means for you.

In the coming chapters, I'll be inviting you to ask difficult questions about your current relationship with money and work, and whether that relationship is defined by your own values or those you've believed because you've simply been taught to—by school, by society, and yes, by your own social circles. Every part of this book is aimed at moving you away from a mindset informed by hustle-culture capitalism and girlboss consumerism, and toward a more abundant, intentional, enriching life.

Keep in mind that this book is meant to provide

FIRE Bro (n.):
a specific type of member of the "financial independence/retire early" community, who sees personal finance as a game you can win by eliminating spending on anything that could possibly be seen as frivolous; sits in judgment of how others waste their money while choosing to suffer through ramen for the sixth day in a row so he can *maybe* stay on track toward retiring by thirty-five

you the tools you need to level up your own relationship with money, and it will do so while addressing the difficult systemic issues that have left many of us out of the game for too long. But the completely unfair truth is that we can't fix poverty and injustice on a personal level. Millennials are the first generation in many to be worse off than their parents, thanks to a student debt crisis, rising living costs that our country's stagnant wages can't keep up with, and the undoing of fundamental rights our parents grew up with (and Gen Z is certainly on the same trajectory). We at TFD will support political candidates and grassroots efforts doing the work to implement social safety nets like universal healthcare, free college, and fair disability benefits, because we believe these things are rights, not privileges. We've implemented fair workplace practices where possible, such as a comprehensive paid maternity leave policy for our employees, six weeks' PTO, and a four-day workweek. But even if every one of us had those safety nets we deserve access to (and we do deserve them), you are still going to be the one in charge of your personal finances, and of advocating for yourself.

So in this book, you will not find quick fixes or false promises for undoing the impact of a system that favors the few over the many. What you will find is advice on how to redefine your worth beyond a job or a number in your bank account, and how to make incremental changes *within your control* to help foster a better quality of life for yourself and others around you.

Throughout the following pages, you'll find plenty of interactive exercises to help you reevaluate everything from your spending habits to your work-life boundaries to how you define your own value. These activities may be straightforward, but that doesn't mean they're *easy*.

This is not a thirty-day challenge to get your money under control for good, and this is not a one-stop series of hacks to get rich quick. Rather, this book will help you define money and work philosophies you can carry with conviction and confidence. Plus, the entire thing has been thoughtfully and beautifully designed by my colleague and TFD's co-founder, Lauren Ver Hage.

Think of utilizing this book the way you do your favorite cookbooks: referring to the well-marked and smudged pages as often as they call to you, knowing you may have to try a recipe a bunch of times before committing the steps to memory and then improvising on them. Because moving beyond getting by isn't something you'll challenge yourself to once—it's something you'll practice for the rest of your life.

FILL ME IN

Prompts to Guide Your Reading

Below you'll find some guiding questions I'd like you to reflect on, but don't think about them too hard beforehand—write the first response that comes to mind. Then, keep your answers in the back of your mind as you work your way through the rest of this book!

When looking at your current financial strategy, what's working? What needs improvement?

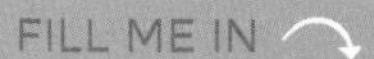

Do you find yourself satisfied with most of the choices you make on a day-to-day basis? Why or why not?

If you could have one extra hour each day, how would you spend it?

FILL ME IN

In order to feel more in control of your own decisions, what in your life needs to change?

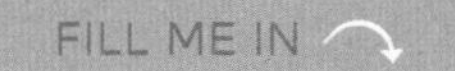

If you had to define yourself by something not work-related, what would it be? Are you content with that answer?

2

MASTERING THE ART OF DE-SHAMING YOUR FINANCES

When you think about being "good with money," what's the first thing that comes to mind? Before I started thinking about the role of money in our lives for my job, I can tell you that *I* always associated it with spending as little as possible. Splurging on a frivolous night out or treating yourself to an extra lipstick meant you didn't have self-control. Being above silly material indulgences made you "good," and giving in to spending temptations meant you were "bad."

Of course, this way of thinking about money doesn't work the way we hope it will. If your financial philosophy is one of constant deprivation, you're bound to get frustrated, "give in" to the spending you were trying to avoid, feel ashamed that you couldn't stick to your plan, and eventually give up entirely. It's the same reason fad diets don't work, at least in the long run. That's exactly why TFD carries "diet" in its title: A diet simply refers to the food you eat, regardless of whether or not it's for a certain end goal. And the only kind of diet that actually works is one that doesn't leave you feeling deprived.

But it's no surprise that this way of approaching money has such a choke hold on American culture. I would argue that the way we're taught to view many things (from money to sexuality to gender expression) is rooted in the shame-based Puritan ideals that colonizers brought with them from Europe. And if we're talking about fear- and shame-based money advice, we simply can't have that conversation without bringing up Dave Ramsey.

Dave Ramsey, American Evangelicalism, and Shame-Based Personal Finance

Dave Ramsey is one of the most (if not *the* most) well-known names in the personal finance media world. According to his company's mission statement, "Ramsey Solutions provides biblically based, commonsense education and empowerment that give HOPE to everyone in every walk of life." He has programs like Financial Peace University that help people get out of debt and build wealth, and he's helped popularize strategies like the debt snowball method.

His company has also faced its fair share of controversies over the years, mostly surrounding the company's faith-based practices. In 2021, a former employee filed a lawsuit against Ramsey Solutions alleging that he was fired over insisting on working remotely during the height of the pandemic. The only advice from his superiors during this time was to simply "pray and keep moving forward," while employees were allegedly being required to continue showing up at the office. The company settled a separate lawsuit in 2022 after a former employee alleged that she was forced to resign after coming out as a lesbian and openly discussing her sexuality at work.

As someone who's worked in this field for years, I've had run-ins with Dave Ramsey's financial worldview at least a few hundred times at this point, from receiving dozens of story pitches dissecting his advice to witnessing debates about his methods in our own YouTube comments section. And I'd be lying if I said his money advice, like his "baby steps" for getting your money in order, hasn't been useful for many people—it definitely has.

But he has also founded his entire personal finance empire on the same ethos as the Evangelical belief system he belongs to: shaming people into making certain lifestyle decisions in order to fit into a very narrow idea of what being "good" looks like. Here is what he preaches:

- **Never taking on any debt, even recommending paying cash for a car instead of getting financing.**
- **Never using a credit card, even giving tips on how to navigate American life without a credit score (spoiler alert: it's deeply complicated).**
- **And never, ever spending a dime on anything fun if you're in the middle of paying off debt.**

Ramsey is just one example of how Evangelical Christian beliefs are deeply ingrained in our relationship with money. America was founded under a puritanical ideology, which viewed poverty as an abject moral failing and wealth as a gift from God. And that has trickled down into present-day Evangelicalism: Largely (and contrary to some specific teachings in the Bible), Evangelical Christians view poverty as an individual issue, not a systemic one.

One of my all-time favorite Ramsey quotes: "If you're working on paying off debt, the only time you should see the inside of a restaurant is if you're working there." For him, rest and indulgence are things you must earn, not rights that should come with being human. (No offense, Dave, but no one deserves to unwind in a restaurant more than service workers themselves.)

Of course, it would be an overgeneralization to say that *every* born-again Christian shares the same beliefs. But a 2017 study performed by *The Washington Post* and the Kaiser Family Foundation (not related to healthcare company Kaiser Permanente) found that Christians, and white Evangelical Christians in particular, are more likely to view poverty as the result of individual failure. The poll found that "46 percent of all Christians said that a lack of effort is generally to blame for a person's poverty, compared with 29 percent of all non-Christians. The gulf widens further among specific Christian groups: 53 percent of white evangelical Protestants blamed lack of effort while 41 percent blamed circumstances, and 50 percent of Catholics blamed lack of effort while 45 percent blamed circumstances. In contrast, by more than 2 to 1, Americans who are atheist, agnostic or have no particular affiliation said difficult circumstances are more to blame when a person is poor than lack of effort (65 percent to 31 percent)."

For literal decades, so much personal finance advice (whether or not it comes from an actual born-again Christian like Ramsey) has echoed the same sentiment: Being poor is simply a result of you, as an individual, not putting in the work needed to change your situation. Personal finance, under this view, is simply a matter of personal responsibility. Ramsey and his counterparts do not allow room for nuance when it comes to money, not once taking into account how our policies and social structures perpetuate cycles of poverty. But that type of shame-based, pull-yourself-up-by-the-bootstraps rhetoric, which leaves no space for acknowledging how society and capitalism are stacked against so many of us, isn't just tired; for most people, it simply doesn't work.

Why Shame-Based Budgeting Fails

In order to explain the role of shame in our collective relationship with money, I reached out to friend of TFD Lindsay Bryan-Podvin, a licensed master social worker, financial therapist, and founder of Mind Money Balance, LLC. Lindsay practices "shame-free financial therapy," which means she approaches personal finance from a place of total empathy and rejects the idea that any "frivolous" spending should be avoided.

"Using shame as a tool to create change is a terrible idea," she says. "Shame is an internalized feeling that we are bad, broken, or unworthy. It directly impacts our perception of our self-worth and esteem. Feeling bad about ourselves because of shame can cause a negative feedback loop, making it incredibly difficult to elicit the behavior change we want. On top of that, research has shown that women are more susceptible to feeling shame more quickly than men and, thus, are more likely to experience its negative impact."

Where the Dave Ramseys of the personal finance world want to shame those of us trying to get better with money out of spending on anything "frivolous," from a treat from Sephora to a weekend getaway,

Bootstrapping (n.):
a belief, often held by conservatives and libertarians, that one person's financial failures and successes are determined by them alone, conveniently ignoring systemic factors that favor a very few

Lindsay acknowledges that this is both unrealistic and harmful. Say a person wants to reduce the amount they spend on restaurants but has followed the advice of a shame-based personal finance creator, and thus has internalized the idea that that kind of spending makes them "bad" or "stupid." What's bound to happen if they go out one time for a happy hour, even though they made it the whole week without restaurant spending? According to Lindsay, "They are smacked in the face with shame, thinking, 'I have no discipline and shouldn't even bother trying to save. What's the point?' They've already decided it's not worth it to try to make a behavior change, so they text their colleagues to see if anyone wants to do Saturday brunch because they've already 'blown' their spending plan." A person budgeting from a place of compassion, however, is equipped to handle the situation in a more balanced way. As Lindsay says:

> **"Instead of being smacked in the face with guilt, their internal dialogue might sound like, 'Holy sh*t! I made it a full workweek without dining out! That happy hour was a treat, and I was much more present because it was the first time I ate out this week, and knew I could afford it. Even though I was trying to cut out dining out, I think cutting back is more sustainable.'"**

It's the same ethos as intuitive eating: Nothing is off-limits, and you honor your health by making mindful choices that genuinely make you feel good.

When prioritizing your long-term financial health, your budget *shouldn't* come from a place of internalized shame. Budgeting this way makes you believe that you must be broke or poor because you're lazy, incompetent, or otherwise undeserving of money. This in turn makes you feel bad about every single "unnecessary" expense. Truthfully, I don't care what you spend your discretionary budget on. I have my own stances about fast fashion and "Instagram worthy" vacations (and trust me, you will hear about them), but when it comes down to your own budget, there are only a few *actually important* things:

- **Pay all your bills on time.**
- **Don't go into debt funding your lifestyle.**
- **Invest in your long-term financial goals.**

On some level, most of us are going to have to use a budget for the rest of our lives. That's an annoying thought—what's the point of getting good with money if you must keep thinking about it? But if you've reached for this book, chances are you know your way around a budget spreadsheet. Maybe you've even worked your way through Dave Ramsey's ~~fearmongering admonishments~~ financial bootcamp, but you're thinking, *Hey, maybe there's a better way*. You're likely past the financial hand-holding phase, and you don't need me to rattle on about the importance of tracking your spending or using a budgeting app to get started. That doesn't mean you have it all figured out, or there's nothing else you can do with your money. It just means you've mastered this one very basic building block and it's time to address the most important thing: whether your short-term spending fits with your long-term goals.

FILL ME IN

Reflection Activity: De-Shaming Your Money Beliefs

Use the space on the next page to rewrite the shame-based money beliefs you're currently holding. Here's an example of my own:

Shame-based belief:
If my husband and I had saved more money, we could have owned a home in the city by now. Every year we continue to rent, we are just throwing away money.

Shame-free revision:
Not owning a home yet means we have been able to prioritize other money goals, like maxing out our retirement contributions. Our rent affords us an apartment we love, and we're lucky enough to live somewhere rent-stabilized so that our spending stays relatively consistent from year to year.

FILL ME IN

SHAME-BASED BELIEFS

SHAME-FREE REVISIONS

Id, Ego, and Superego: The Only Three Budget Categories You Need

One of my favorite budgeting methods to help people start is the 50/30/20 budget, or 50/30/20 rule. (This was popularized in the book *All Your Worth: The Ultimate Lifetime Money Plan*, written by Elizabeth Warren and her daughter—honestly, if there's one politician I would trust with my personal finances, it's Warren.) The method is very simple: You take your after-tax income, or your take-home pay, and divide it into three categories: 50% to needs, 30% to wants, and 20% to financial goals.

Of course, this is simply one way to create a *big-picture* plan for your budget; it's not a set of hard-and-fast rules for determining how much you're allowed to spend on clothes and how to spend as little as possible on groceries, etc. If anything in finance gives Ramsey vibes, it is nitpicky rules that don't make sense for most people. (I once read that you should aim to spend exactly 5% of your income on clothing. Who is that helping?)

The 50/30/20 rule is a way to assess whether you are living within your means; however, the numbers themselves can be a bit constricting. Many Americans cannot afford to spend less than 50% of their take-home

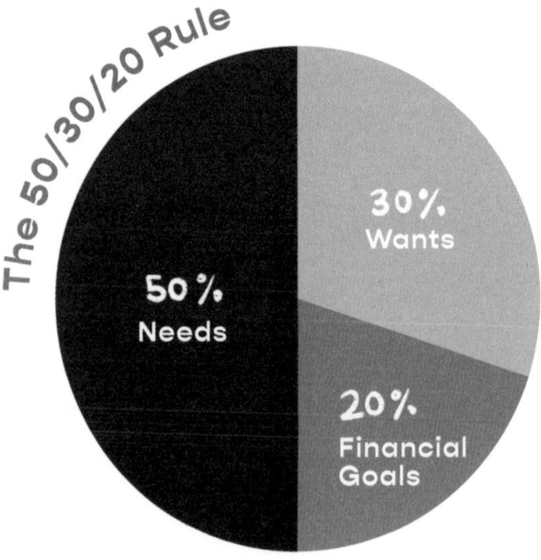

pay on necessities (she writes from the apartment in Brooklyn with a rent that's more than her parents' mortgage payment for a suburban Atlanta ranch).

Instead, I want to take it a bit Freudian (but not in a gross way) and ask you to think of your budget in these more fluid terms:

- **Ego:** Spend an ***affordable*** amount on your needs
- **Superego:** Save ***enough*** for your financial goals
- **Id:** Spend ***what's left*** of your budget on wants

As long as you are able to fit your budget within these parameters, you don't have to worry about the specifics—it's a way to budget so you (almost) never have to think about your budget.

The Financial Ego: Affording the Basics

In psychoanalytic theory (stay with me), the ego is the part of the self that acts as a regulator. It prevents you from giving in too much to your baser desires, but it also keeps your hypervigilant, perfectionist tendencies in check. When it comes to your finances, the ego encompasses your baseline needs—the expenses you simply could not go without. Think your rent or mortgage, healthcare/prescriptions, childcare or other caretaker costs, transportation, utilities, cellphone/internet, groceries, and anything else you couldn't cut from your budget, even in an emergency situation. (This is an important reminder that everything is negotiable, including and especially things like your monthly bills.)

Now, if we're following the traditional 50/30/20 budget, you would add up your entire household monthly take-home pay, multiply it by 0.5, and come up with the number that (in an ideal situation) should be able to cover all of your necessities in a given month. If you do this and you find you're already keeping your necessities below 50%, you're doing amazing, sweetie, and you can head to the next section.

But as I mentioned, limiting necessary spending to 50% of after-tax income is quite literally impossible for many people, in America and elsewhere. The cost of living throughout the country is so variable, and in many places, wages just haven't kept up. As long as the rest of your budget allows you to live well—that is, you're able to set aside enough money for your long-term goals, and you don't feel deprived of "fun" spending—spending 60%, or potentially even more, on your financial ego isn't a dealbreaker.

In 2007, Congress voted to increase the federal minimum wage for the first time in ten years, bringing it from $5.15 to $7.25. As of this writing, it has yet to be increased again, sixteen years later.

But if you're struggling to work toward your financial goals, and you *do* feel deprived of enough just-for-fun spending, you essentially have two options: You cut down your necessary expenses or you start earning more so you can afford them. (I'll cover that plenty later on in this book.)

The Financial Superego: Learning to Love Delayed Gratification

Taking it back to Dr. Freud, the superego is the part of the self that acts as our personal moral compass, always aiming to be perfect despite what pulls us in other directions. Translating this to personal finances, it is the part of your budget that takes care of the money tasks that center on delayed gratification, i.e., your long-term financial goals. Setting money aside for these goals rarely feels fun in the moment, but you know it's good for you over time.

This is the most important part of your big-picture budget. This book is about learning to live abundantly in every aspect of your life, and you can't truly feel abundance if you're constantly worried about your current and future financial security. Of course, the parameters of your specific financial superego will depend on your own circumstances, from your long-term goals to your family situation, and they will likely change over time. Your financial goals will range from paying off debt, to building up an emergency fund, to contributing to your retirement account, to saving for a down payment, to planning for your children's education.

If you were following the 50/30/20 rule, you'd want to aim for putting 20% of your income toward your financial goals, but that ultimately depends entirely on what your goals are. The important thing is not so much the specific percentage, but that you're contributing enough to reach your goals. In a few chapters, we'll cover how to determine what should make up your own financial superego, including learning the right amount to save or invest toward these objectives.

The Financial Id: Finding Your IDGAF Number

Now on to the most exciting part of your big-picture budget: your financial id. The id is the childish part of the self that wants to do whatever it wants, whenever it wants, without any care for the consequences. In your budget, this translates to anything that is not absolutely essential. That doesn't mean your financial id will be made up of illicit substances or nights at the bar till 3:00 A.M. Your "indulgent" spending may very well be made up of one-on-one Pilates sessions and expensive jams from the farmers' market. (Maybe some combo of the above? I'm not judging.)

It doesn't matter what makes up your id, or how indulgent it appears to other people. Just be honest with yourself about what is, in fact, a want and not a need. Transportation is a need—taking Ubers places you could easily reach on the subway is a want. Clothing is a need—having a new outfit every time you take a TikTok video is a want. Groceries are a need—ordering grocery delivery as an able-bodied, single, child-free person is, I'm sorry, a want. (And so help me, if you're not tipping your delivery person, a tiny dose of shame may actually be in order; maybe jump ahead to the chapter on being cheap.)

This is not to scare you out of spending on any of those things; you just have to be mindful of the fact that a dollar spent on a want is a dollar that's not going toward your financial future. Again, as long as you're still able to meet your basic needs and contribute what you need to your long-term goals, the specifics don't really matter. Think of your id as an "IDGAF number"; your household take-home pay minus your needs and goals spending equals the amount that can go toward whatever else you want each month. You just need to keep that number in your head (or in a budgeting spreadsheet or app), not spend over it in a given month, and you're golden.

Moving Beyond Shame-Based Budgeting

Dave Ramsey is simply one of a host of personalities who typify the puritanical American view that failing financially means you're failing as a person. He doesn't believe that poor people deserve to experience the joys of the present until they've paid off every last penny of debt and therefore earned the right to do so.

But when you are planning your finances from a place of shame and deprivation, you're not allowing yourself to view all of your needs *and* wants as essential to creating a whole, healthy life. Spending all your energy and every dollar on the future means you're unable to care about the present, and while you deserve to take care of your future self, your current self deserves attention, too. On the other hand, you can't be only focused on the present, or both your current and future selves would suffer—the very definition of simply *getting by*. Budgeting should be a tool you utilize to live more abundantly, because you deserve to take care of every aspect of yourself.

Moving beyond getting by means getting to a place where your budget is something you rarely think about, because you've mastered the practicalities of financial management—and they really aren't very hard, I promise—and can actually focus on living your life. At the end of the day, money is simply a tool, and the entire point of being good with it is so that you don't have to think about it as its own objective. Shame has no place in the equation.

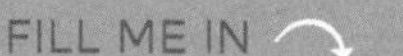

Categorizing Your Financial Ego, Superego, and Id

Use the pie chart below to categorize your current expenses in your financial ego, superego, and id. Remember that these numbers are fluid and will necessarily change over time—especially as you work through the rest of this book and start reevaluating your priorities.

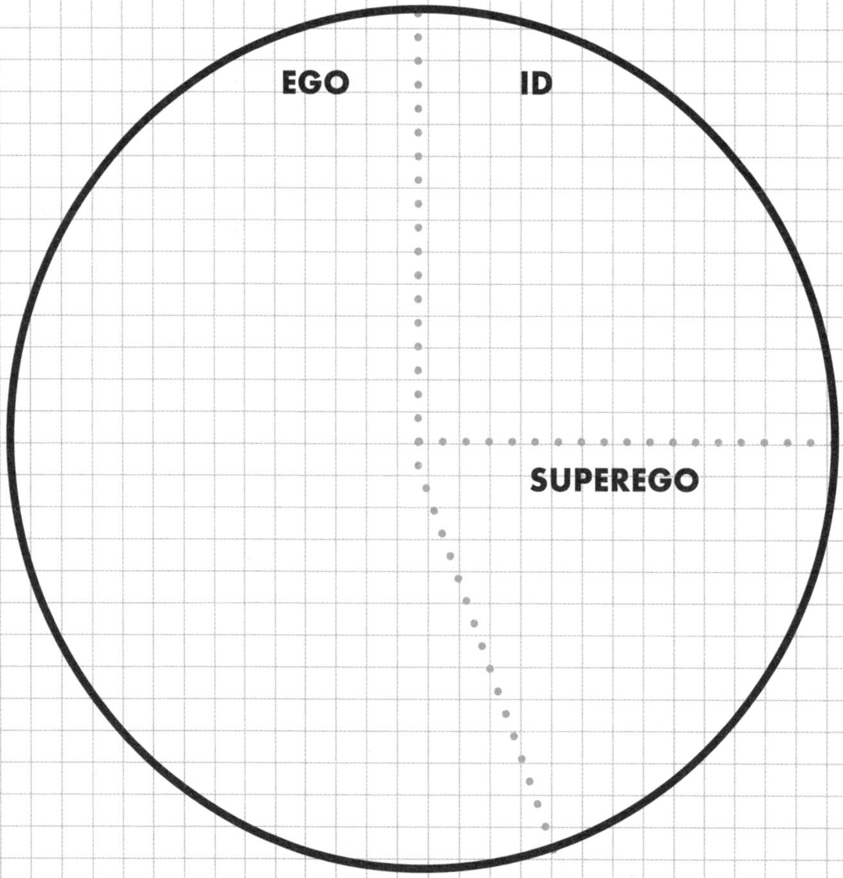

EGO

ID

SUPEREGO

3

THE CONTRADICTORY TRUTH OF THE "HAPPINESS THRESHOLD"

Here's a reality check before I dive into this chapter: Having basically anything in savings is an immense privilege. Almost half of Americans can't afford to cover a $500 emergency. If we're telling these same people to look at budgeting strategies like the 50/30/20 rule in order to get their money right, how can we expect them to keep their essential spending under 50%, or even 60%, of their take-home pay, when they're barely able to cover the necessities in the first place?

So much money advice—even the good advice—centers around saving money by cutting back your spending, which can be genuinely helpful. But it is also geared toward people who have something to start with, in the sense that they haven't already cut their spending to the bare minimum. Maybe you can start growing your own vegetables to save money on groceries in the long run, or you can take in a roommate to cover some of your mortgage or rent, or you can move to a place with lower taxes. But each of these assumes you have the privilege to be able to make the changes in the first place, like enough outdoor space for a garden, a home with a spare room, or a remote job and enough cash that you can simply decide it's time to get up and move.

Things like more space and extra money are privileges because they mean you're starting a few steps ahead. But unfortunately, many people *are* starting from zero—and it's a lot harder to move beyond making ends meet when you don't have anything left to cut from your budget. While I would much rather see our social safety net expanded so that no one has to forgo the possibility of a stable retirement because they simply can't afford to think beyond today, I know that can't happen overnight. Because while setting up a shame-free budget plan is something we can all do to live better with what we have, the reality is that you can cut your financial ego, or your necessary expenses, only so much in order to make room for the superego and id of your finances—your long-term goals and just-for-fun spending.

This chapter is all about defining your own happiness threshold and avoiding the trap of lifestyle inflation, but only take this advice if it's available to you. If you have nothing left to cut from your budget, or you aren't in a place where you're able to focus on earning more, remember that is in no way a reflection of your value as a person.

But once you *are* able to focus on either increasing your income or decreasing your expenses, how do you decide what is "enough"? What is the ultimate point of earning more, and how do you decide what you need?

The Elusive Happiness Threshold

The "happiness threshold" has been a viral topic in the media over the past several years. The argument goes that, up to a certain income level, happiness increases. Beyond that threshold, supposedly, more income brings diminishing returns when it comes to happiness. And researchers have been downright obsessed with trying to assign a dollar amount to this concept.

The "happiness threshold":
the idea that money *can* buy you happiness, but only up to a certain point; one now-famous study claimed that happiness tops out at a salary of about $75,000 a year, while others have claimed the range is $80,000–$200,000, depending on which state you live in

But the idea that there's one ultimate number everyone needs to aspire to earn in order to be happy ignores our individual needs and circumstances. It would be reductive to assume that a married mother of two living in Nebraska has the same personal happiness threshold as a single, child-free woman in Manhattan. They'd have different income needs informed by both their cost of living and their responsibilities—not to mention their different values and interests.

The question of *what* makes us happier, though, is one that many behavioral scientists and researchers have been trying to answer for a long time now. As part of the Harvard Study of Adult Development, one of the longest studies of adult life in the world, researchers followed a group of men (and eventually their offspring) for over eighty years. They found one overwhelming factor that predicted long and happy lives: close relationships. A different report, from the *Journal of Personality and Social Psychology*, found autonomy, "the feeling that your life—its activities and habits—are self-chosen and self-endorsed," to be the key factor in determining happiness. Happiness expert Gretchen Rubin has dedicated over a decade of her life to researching what makes us most content, and she says there are two main factors that contribute to greater happiness: strong relationships and being self-aware. As she told CNBC, "Knowing yourself involves knowing your own interests, values, and temperament. Once you know that, you can build your life around the things that are true for you instead of what you wish were true or what other people expect from you."

Research-Driven Factors for Happiness:

- ✶ Investing in close relationships
- ✶ Self-awareness
- ✶ Personal autonomy

Investing in your close relationships, understanding and acting on your own values, and having control over your choices: While these things don't come with a specific *cost*, they are not totally divorced from money, because they each require time and energy. For instance, in order to invest in your relationships, it's helpful to have a steady, reliable source of income that doesn't require you to work excessive overtime. It's a lot easier to change career paths or make another big personal decision when you have enough cushion to do so comfortably, which could be from an emergency fund, help from family, a partner with a steady income, etc. And living by your priorities and values, like dining at local restaurants or investing in travel, is a lot more feasible when you have resources like wiggle room in your budget or ample paid time off.

The idea of the happiness threshold is an oversimplification, but it does take these factors into account. Because up to a certain point, having more time and more options *can* make you happier—but not necessarily past that point.

Why Rich People Are Miserable

It would make sense to think that the ultra-rich should be happier than the rest of us, because they have the time and resources to focus on those factors we've determined make people happy—close relationships, being in control of their choices, spending on things and experiences that align with their values and interests. So why do many rich people seem so unhappy?

If social connections are a key factor for happiness, the rich are failing miserably. In a 2016 study analyzing results from the General Social Survey and the American Time Use Survey, researchers found that, on average, people with higher incomes spend ten minutes more by themselves every day than people with lower incomes, as well as twenty-six minutes less per day with family.

Rich people also tend to surround themselves with other rich people. A 2014 study that randomly assigned research participants with online chat partners from various socioeconomic backgrounds found that "participants were less interested in spending time and becoming friends with the person when the profile described a cross-class partner, compared to a same-class partner. This was especially true of upper-class participants, who were much less interested in engaging with a lower-class person than with an upper-class counterpart."

And when you self-select your way out of spending time with people from a less-privileged background, you corrode your capacity for empathy—a key ingredient to building and maintaining relationships, one of the main factors for happiness. Friendships last when they are built on empathy, because each participant feels equally able to share emotions and vulnerabilities, thus fostering deeper connections. Yet a study published in *Psychological Science* found that, after conducting a series of experiments, people from lower socioeconomic classes were better at reading others' facial expressions than people from higher socioeconomic classes—an important measure of what researchers refer to as "empathetic accuracy":

> **"Lower-class environments are much different from upper-class environments," explains Michael Kraus, the study's co-author. "Lower-class individuals have to respond chronically to a number of vulnerabilities and social threats. You really need to depend on others so they will tell you if a social threat or opportunity is coming and that makes you more perceptive of emotions."**

Maintaining fulfilling relationships and being able to depend on others isn't inherently limited to people of lower social classes, of course. But when you

According to data from the General Social Survey and the American Time Use Survey, in the course of a year, rich people are missing out on the equivalent of 6.5 *full days* with their families, when compared with people from lower income brackets.

can take care of any problem by throwing money at it, you may close yourself off from fulfilling relationships. More money gives you more options to self-isolate, from outsourcing every errand so you can never be inconvenienced, to handing your kids off to a nanny every waking moment. As you start to earn and spend more, maintaining connections becomes a chore you could easily skip (and then eventually find yourself surrounded by people who are paid to be there, rather than people you have organic connections with). We see this dynamic echoed in fiction as much as in real life. For every depressed Kendall Roy trying to fill an emotional void by acquiring a "woke" media company and spending all his time away from his children, there's an Elon Musk on child number twenty-seven from girlfriend number twelve . . . occasionally also acquiring a woke media company.

When the "Golden Handcuffs" Start Rusting

When rich people are isolated from the average person's experience, and even from their own families, it's often by their own design, and part of this can be attributed to the addictive power of wealth. Money addiction falls under the class of "process addictions," which also includes things like sex addiction and gambling addiction—out-of-control or compulsive behaviors that form around activities rather than substances. As clinical psychologist Dr. Tian Dayton wrote in *HuffPost*, these addictions, like constantly trying to earn more money, "can [kick-start] the release of brain/body chemicals, like dopamine, that actually produce a 'high' that's similar to the chemical high of a drug. The person who is addicted to some form of behavior has learned, albeit unconsciously, to manipulate his own brain chemistry."

Some money-related process addictions, like gambling or shopping addictions, are well studied; the World Health Organization estimates that gambling addiction affects up to 6% of the population, and other research shows that nearly 5% of adults suffer from shopping addiction. Unfortunately, there's not as much research available on the addictive power of wealth. But here are some negative consequences that researchers tend to associate with behavioral addiction:

- being withdrawn and isolated
- having poor social and romantic relationships
- experiencing mental health issues
- having issues with work or school

This isn't to dismiss the mental and emotional impacts of poverty, and the point here is not to assert that being rich is the worst thing that can happen to you. It is simply to demonstrate that acquiring more wealth for the sake of it is not necessarily a healthy or worthwhile pursuit—it's not what will make you happy, and it can often have the opposite effect. Not to mention, narrowing your social circles warps your perception of what "normal" looks like and can create the perception of not having enough when you actually have plenty. It's the entire reason people run into trouble trying to "keep up with the Joneses."

And when you get accustomed to the compensation from a cushy corporate law, finance, or other high-paying job, the financial incentive of staying, no matter how soul-sucking it is, is very difficult to give up. When you know what earning $300,000, $400,000, even $500,000 a year can get you, opting to go with less feels like self-deprivation. This is what's known as the "golden handcuffs," a classic tale leading to lifestyle inflation: letting your spending increase as your income increases. The more you live at or above your means, the more you are going to think you "need" in order to be happy. It can trap you in a career that you don't actually like, one that may even go against your values, simply because your brain has been

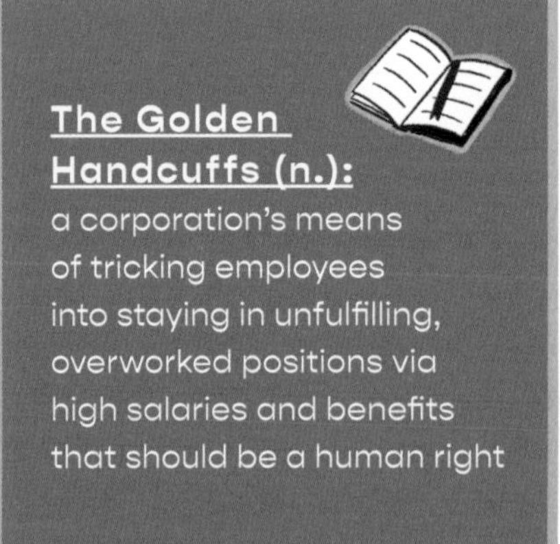

The Golden Handcuffs (n.): a corporation's means of tricking employees into staying in unfulfilling, overworked positions via high salaries and benefits that should be a human right

tricked into thinking what you need for base-level happiness is actually much, much more than reality. The key to defining your own happiness threshold is to have ample clarity on what you need and what "extra" spending is genuinely going to improve your life.

Defining Your Own Happiness Threshold

All of this doesn't mean you can't, or shouldn't, aspire to earn more. Determining how much you want to earn, and therefore how much you'll be able to spend and save, is going to depend on your specific circumstances, which certainly can't be boiled down to a statistic—whether or not you are married or single, have kids or other dependents, are supporting a colony of aloof but beautiful feral cats, etc. In order to live a life where you don't have to constantly be worrying about your budget, you need to be able to live effortlessly below your means. And for that to happen, you might need to earn more—but you might also need to reevaluate what constitutes your "needs."

When I asked Lindsay Bryan-Podvin to share her thoughts on defining your own happiness threshold, she said she prefers an "enoughness" threshold that's based on spending within your values:

> **"If sustainability, community, and connectedness are a person's core values, are their spending habits aligned with those values? A 'yes' might look like getting a CSA box, reducing takeout to a few times per month, and prioritizing get-togethers with friends. A 'no' might look like Amazon-Priming things several times per week, buying more food than needed and contributing to food waste, and avoiding community opportunities for connection."**

FILL ME IN

Clarifying Your Financial Values

When it's time to interrogate your own financial values, start with the driving force behind certain spending habits. In cognitive behavioral therapy, clarifying your values is an exercise that involves creating a personal hierarchy of beliefs so that a patient can make decisions based on those values and create a better quality of life for themselves.

This exercise will help you clarify your personal values, which will in turn inform how you categorize various lifestyle decisions (nonnegotiables, valuable bonuses, indifferent additions)—by how much they contribute to your overall happiness:

First, determine your broader core values by circling up to ten of those listed below (or list your own in the fill-in-the-blank spaces) based on what's most important to you.

Active Lifestyle

Alone Time

Altruism

Arts & Entertainment

Career Advancement

Caregiving

Community Engagement

Creative Expression

Cultural Enrichment

Dining Experiences

Education/Lifelong Learning

Entertaining/Hosting

Environmentalism

Family

Flexibility

Free Time

Friendships

Home Cooking

FILL ME IN

Home Life

Leadership

New Experiences

Outdoor Recreation

Personal Development

Physical Fitness

Political Activism

Religion/Spirituality

Responsibility

Routine & Structure

Sports

Travel

Urbanism

Variety

Other:

______________________ ______________________

______________________ ______________________

______________________ ______________________

______________________ ______________________

______________________ ______________________

______________________ ______________________

______________________ ______________________

Then, write your top three values from this selection in the space below.

1. ______________________________________

2. ______________________________________

3. ______________________________________

Matching Your Financial Decisions with Your Values

Living (and spending) in a way that's aligned with your values is key to living a more abundant, more intentional, and overall more joyful life. But much of the time, we don't assess our spending mindfully. So, when determining your own happiness threshold, that's the best place to start: Are your current money habits aligned with your personal values and interests?

My own come-to-Jesus moment, in terms of lifestyle inflation, happened when I started paying attention to what I was spending on Ubers and Lyfts. One of my biggest personal values is maintaining a lifestyle that is not car-dependent, and I am privileged enough to live in a place where this is possible. I love that I live in an extremely walkable neighborhood and have plenty of easy access to public transportation. So why was I spending hundreds of dollars a month on ride-hailing apps? (The answer is laziness.) Sometimes calling a car is the faster option, but not always—traffic in New York is often much worse than our subway slowdowns, and at least on the subway, I get ample time alone with my Kindle and endless supply of library ebooks. I also value being active, am lucky to be able-bodied, and enjoy walking. Defaulting to taking a car whenever I was mildly inconvenienced was deteriorating my relationship to my community and causing me to live a less active lifestyle along the way. It was a luxury, but I was treating it like a necessity, and therefore giving myself less money to spend on things that were more aligned with my values.

Reminder:
One person's luxury is another person's necessity. For me, using ride-sharing apps is the former, but for people with limited mobility, it could very well be the latter. And that's just one example!

Of course, your happiness threshold is not going to remain stagnant. For one thing, your life is going to change, regardless of how in control you feel. Maybe you'll have kids or end up being a primary caregiver for a family member, or suddenly need to move, or God forbid, find yourself living through *another* pandemic that positions your dog as your only social outlet for months on end. But even if your own life somehow never changes, inflation is bound to happen. And for Americans, life gets considerably more expensive every year—3.8% on average since the sixties, and almost double that in 2022. What you need to earn to cover your happiness threshold now may look totally different ten years from now, or even next year.

But when you look at that list of values, remember that it's not just your money that determines whether you're able to live by them: It's also your time. The entire purpose of increasing your income should be to aim for *more* flexibility, not less. Taking on a job that pays a high salary but erodes your free time would be counterproductive. And instead of thinking of your happiness

What is inflation? According to the International Monetary Fund, "inflation" refers to "how much more expensive a set of goods and services has become over a certain period, usually a year." On a personal level, it's why your gas or your groceries suddenly cost so much more than they did last year. It happens when demand is outweighing supply—for instance, when housing prices skyrocketed in certain markets in 2020 and 2021, it was because many more people wanted to buy than there were houses available.

threshold as one immovable number, think of it as something to schedule for yearly maintenance, like a doctor's appointment. When you go in for your scheduled maintenance, it's time to reassess whether your spending habits and what you do with your time are currently in line with what you value.

FILL ME IN

Your Happiness Threshold Check-In

Referring back to your list of core values, write down your current spending in the boxes below. Any spending that aligns with your top three core values will go in the "Prioritize First" column. Spending that aligns with your remaining top ten core values will go in the "Prioritize Second" column. And any spending that doesn't align with your core values can go in the "De-prioritize" column.

Broad spending category:	**Prioritize first:** What spending is *nonnegotiable* for your happiness in this category?	**Prioritize second:** What spending is *nice to have* for your happiness in this category?	**De-prioritize:** What spending are you *indifferent* to in this category?
Housing & transportation			
Food (groceries & dining)			
Family & social fulfillment			
Hobbies & leisure time			
Clothing & other material goods			

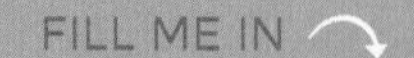

Does your current income allow you to cover the spending in the first two columns, in addition to covering your essentials and long-term goals (your financial ego and superego)?

If not, how much more do you think you need to bring in to hit that level of contentment?

FILL ME IN

Does your current schedule allow you the free time you need to live by those values? Why or why not?

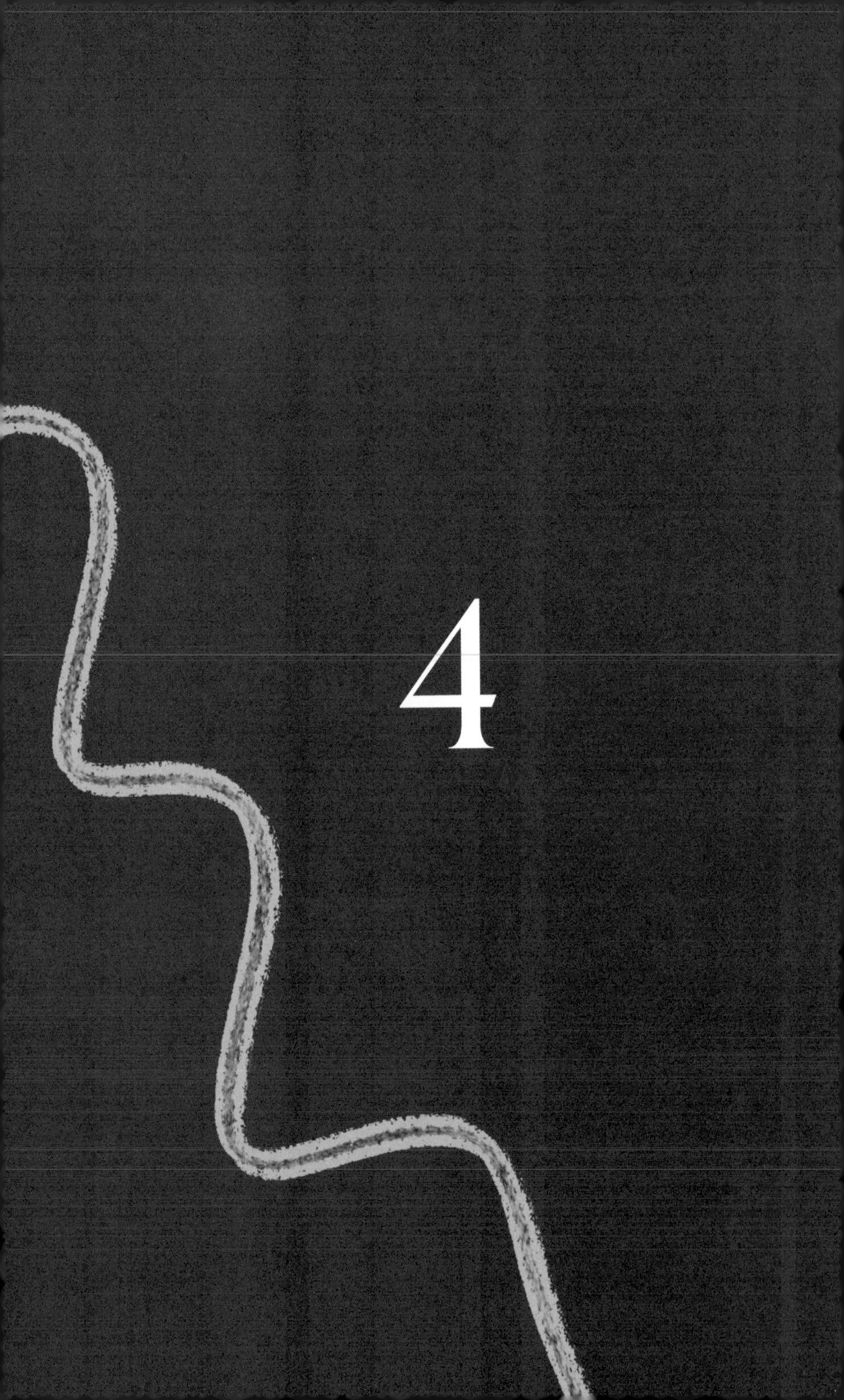

4

FINDING FINANCIAL INDEPENDENCE IN THE ASHES OF THE CRYPTO CRASH

If you picked up this book, chances are you've read the first TFD book or maybe watched your way through our YouTube channel, or at least have some understanding of the basics of investing. You not only know what retirement accounts like a 401(k), 403(b), and IRA are, you have also made sure to enroll in your employer's matching program if one is available to you. Maybe you've even started working with a financial professional (if you're worried about cost, Advisor.com is a great option for making financial planning more accessible) to make your money habits match your goals, and you're (hopefully) already following the advice to put at least 10% of your income toward retirement. You've already built your healthy financial foundation—so what now?

If you actually *don't* have a solid grasp on the basics of investing, that's okay! I'd just recommend doing a little preliminary research before diving into this chapter. Besides the first TFD book, here are some great resources:

* Amanda Holden (aka @dumpster.doggy) on Instagram
* The book *Broke Millennial Takes On Investing* by Erin Lowry
* The book *Your Money or Your Life* by Vicki Robin and Joe Dominguez
* The "Investing" playlist on TFD's YouTube channel

Now is the time to start thinking about your wealth, the biggest piece of your financial superego, more intentionally—and look into options that maybe weren't feasible when you were twenty-two and sneaking Tupperware filled with leftovers out of catered staff meetings to save a few bucks on groceries (or maybe that was just me). And unfortunately, we cannot talk about people taking their wealth-building into their own hands (with sometimes mixed to disastrous results) post-2022 without first talking about crypto.

When I first started working for TFD in September 2016, cryptocurrency was barely on our radar. We avoided covering financial topics that were too niche for our core audience of women who wanted to get better with money simply to live better; we cared about putting accessible advice out there, of course, but the lackluster clicks wouldn't have justified the energy needed to produce the content. Crypto was new, we weren't accredited finance experts, and there was no need to start promoting financial assets that hadn't been proven to hold any real value yet when tried-and-true investing advice would be more than enough for most of our readers and viewers. We already discouraged individual stock picking (and still do), because the average investor is rarely good at beating the market. Crypto was just another opportunity for individuals wading out of their

Crypto Key Terms

Cryptocurrency:
a decentralized digital asset based on a network that is distributed across a large number of computers

Blockchain:
the type of database that is used to record cryptocurrency transactions; because of the way the technology works, it is almost impossible to forge transaction histories, meaning there isn't a concern about easily faking or duplicating crypto transactions—even without being regulated by a trusted intermediary like the government

Bitcoin:
likely the most famous and valuable cryptocurrency, which was introduced to the public in 2009

The greater fool theory asserts that overvalued assets will go up in price when there are enough investors willing to pay more for them; even Bill Gates has disavowed crypto as being rooted in this theory.

NFTs are "non-fungible tokens" that typically take the form of digital art secured by cryptocurrency. Like art, they are assets that hold value and can be seen as investments but aren't themselves currency.

depth to lose money, which is entirely avoidable when there are plenty of more reliable avenues for lucrative investing, like putting your money in low-cost index funds. Besides, Bitcoin and NFTs and "the future of money" were things our readers could be bored hearing about on their bad Tinder dates—they didn't need it from us, too.

But soon it became clear that crypto wasn't something we could categorically ignore on our channels. It wasn't just a niche topic of interest for personal finance geeks and cyber-libertarians who didn't want their online transactions easily trackable by a too-involved government. Crypto was gaining traction, getting coverage on mainstream finance sites, and even becoming tradable on trustworthy finance platforms.

The Crypto Crash: Understanding the Bare Minimum

The way that cryptocurrencies work is this: They increase in value when there's more interest in and demand for them. Generally, their value is inherently speculative and not backed by anything real, so the more people who buy into them, the more valuable they become—and that value can boom overnight. But it also means, as we saw with the market-wide cryptocurrency crash in 2022, that their value can disappear overnight, too.

One of the most important differences between money you're used to spending and cryptocurrency is that fiat currency—which is what

USD is—is backed by a government entity, while crypto is not. The inherent tension with crypto lies in the fact that something can't simultaneously function as both a usable currency and a high-yield investment, yet that's what people have come to expect from crypto.

I am no expert on the crypto crash—nor do you need to be—but it's worth having a basic knowledge of what went down. At the start of 2022, crypto was hot and Bitcoin was more valuable than it had ever been. Paris Hilton even showed up to *The Tonight Show Starring Jimmy Fallon* to marvel at her and Jimmy's Bored Ape NFTs to a bewildered audience (which was later alleged to be part of a vast scheme to artificially inflate the value of Bored Ape NFTs and help line their own pockets). Then, when the Federal Reserve started hiking up interest rates to try to get a hold on inflation, the value of different cryptocurrencies started tanking.

According to Lee Reiners, a teacher of cryptocurrency law at Duke, "The crypto winter also revealed larger, systemic problems in the industry. It really exposed a number of crypto firms who were, you know, overextended, had poor risk management, or otherwise engaging in fraudulent activity." One of the most massive crypto implosions was that of crypto company FTX, which was valued at $32 billion at the beginning of 2022 and was bankrupt by the end of it. The company's founder, Sam Bankman-Fried, used to be seen as a crypto wunderkind, but is now (as of the time of this writing) awaiting trial on counts of wire fraud, conspiracy to commit money laundering, and conspiracy to misuse customer funds, in addition to several other charges.

Now, as I've mentioned, I'm not an investing expert; I certainly wouldn't have been able to predict the crypto bubble bursting in 2022, especially not as quickly and violently as it did.

Crypto Bro (n.):
a man with a tendency to dominate conversations with talk of his latest ill-advised investments; gets especially heated when you compare crypto to a Ponzi scheme; truly just some guy

But plenty of finance experts we *do* trust at TFD saw that coming, or were at least willing to be skeptical about the idea of getting rich off crypto. One of them is Richard Coffin, the CFA and CFP professional behind the YouTube channel The Plain Bagel, where he's been offering balanced arguments against overly optimistic crypto advice for years now. I wanted to get his take on why some people are susceptible to empty promises of unregulated and unprotected financial assets like crypto, and where they should channel that energy instead.

BREAKING DOWN THE CRYPTO MELTDOWN WITH THE PLAIN BAGEL'S RICHARD COFFIN

Why have so many people been susceptible to losing money in the crypto space?

It's the same with a lot of technological revolutions: Tech tends to evolve a lot faster than regulation is able to keep up. The issue is with finance—it's very easy for that to then become a breeding ground for scams, for fraud. And we saw a lot of that with crypto. There were crypto projects popping up left, right, and center, many of them run by individuals (or a team of, at times, teenagers) who really had no interest outside of making a quick buck. Traditional finance had that same issue around the time of the Great Depression. There was a lot of misrepresentation around stocks leading up to the stock crash of 1929. A lot of brokers would overhype the promises of stocks and really had no intention of getting their investors money, just to line their own pockets. And then that led to regulations in terms of who can give financial advice, which has still been a work in progress.

Another part of it is macro headwinds. Twenty twenty-two was a year of very contractionary monetary policies [i.e., policies where the government decides to raise interest rates or cut spending]. So with a negative economic environment, more speculative investments tend to be the first ones to lose money and tend to be the first ones to crash in value.

If cryptocurrencies ever were to be more regulated, do you think they could become something that is worth people actively investing in or using in the future?

There has to be some underlying function. And that's where a lot of these projects lack. A lot of them just create a token for the sake of having a token, but there's no real value being generated. So if we were to see wider adoption of the technology and there's actual value being created, whether it be businesses using tokens to fund their operations or what have you, then maybe we get to that point. But that's going to need regulation and stuff to support and increase confidence in the space, especially after 2022, when a lot of the space has lost a lot of people quite a bit of money.

What advice would you give to someone who feels FOMO (fear of missing out) when they hear about people making tons of money off of crypto, or some other next-big-thing investment? Is it

worth trying to get in on the ground floor of new investments?

What we *have* seen throughout history is that a lot of revolutionary technology is *not a good investment* at the aggregate level. . . . The truth is, there's no room for two thousand different cryptocurrencies over the next decade. There just isn't. And a lot of those are going to go to zero as a result of that. For someone who is feeling FOMO on these big returns, on the one hand, it's reassuring to tell them this isn't the first—and it won't be the last—big rise and fall of something. We saw it with computers. We saw it with the internet. There's always a big revolutionary technology that will make some people a lot of money, but then entice more people to follow it, which tends to lose them money. And at the aggregate level, investors tend to fund revolutionary change with their losses, unfortunately.

It's worth recognizing your own limitations. To get in on the ground floor of something, you often need to be an expert in that area . . . .You wouldn't go buy a racehorse without any experience on the tracks. I don't view stocks as gambling, like horse racing, but you need to recognize where your expertise and experience is. And if it isn't in stock picking, or financial research, then it's self-defeating to put yourself in a position where you're now stock picking or picking cryptocurrency projects based on what's going to blow up. Also, you don't have to get in on the ground floor of anything to make good money from it if it's a truly good investment.

If Not Crypto, Then What?

The only real point of demystifying crypto is to underscore what we at TFD have said about investing for years: A good strategy is usually a boring one. Investing is a long game, and the most important aspects are essentially:

- **Get started as early as you can so your money has ample time to grow.**
- **Make sure you're actually *investing* the money you contribute to your 401(k), 403(b), or IRA, as the accounts are not themselves investments, they just hold investments.**
- **Continue contributing to your retirement regularly throughout your earning years.**

"Retirement," though, is a hugely intimidating concept, especially when it's likely several decades in the future. It can also be difficult to gauge whether you're on the right track, even if you are already investing consistently. Retirement isn't necessarily an age; it's an amount of money. Financial independence means having enough money in the bank to stop working if you want to. There are nuances, of course: Retirement accounts will penalize you for withdrawing before you've reached technical retirement age (fifty-nine and a half), so if you want to walk away from other income before then, you will have to plan for it. And that doesn't even cover the humongous question mark of Social Security, which currently has a withdrawal age of sixty-seven for anyone born after 1960.

And while the average stock market return has been 10% historically, nothing is guaranteed. Therefore, increasing the amount you're able to invest over time is critical. I spoke with Amanda Holden, a former investment manager turned blogger and investing educator (she's even taught some of our most popular digital courses over at TFD!). I've always loved Amanda's advice, because it strikes a perfect balance between flexibility and practicality.

Traditionally, **financial independence** means having enough money to live on without getting income from a job. This could mean living off cash savings or passive income from investments.

When it comes to planning for your own retirement or financial independence, the name of the game is *not* to get too in the weeds—just put as much toward it as you can. "Instead of obsessing over the age-based milestones that most people simply cannot meet, every year I just do my best to increase the gap between my earning and spending and invest the difference," she said. She also encourages her students to visualize the future they want for themselves, because that will play a huge part in motivating them to follow through with their investment plans.

"I like to call my future self my 'Bad Granny' (though yours certainly doesn't have to be bad, or a granny!). Mine will be romping around Europe, eating baguettes in France with her significantly younger lover. This exercise helps us keep a face on the process, which happens to be an adorable and slightly wrinklier version of the face you have now. We don't save and invest and learn about Roth IRAs because we get a kick out of Roth IRAs; we do it for our Bad Grannies."

But Amanda is also quick to note that retirement isn't just about traveling, spending time on hobbies, or sowing your wild middle-aged-to-elderly oats; it's also about taking care of yourself. It is sobering to learn that older women are one of the most affected populations when it comes to living in poverty in this country: 1 in 10 women over sixty-five live below the poverty line, and that number increases among single women and women in marginalized communities. Planning for as robust a retirement as possible means caring for your future self's well-being. And remember, it doesn't matter how long you plan on working. Even if you wanted to work forever (which I hope isn't the case), you never know when a medical emergency will happen that leaves you unable to work, or maybe requires you to quit full-time work to take care of a family member. Investing in your retirement is crucial for keeping your options open.

But again, once you're past the point of starting your contributions, it can be difficult to gauge whether you're saving enough to retire the way you want to. When you think of that "bad granny" life for yourself, what's it going to cost you, and how do you know if you're on track to get there? I asked Amanda to answer some questions about tweaking your strategy, aiming for a solid retirement on an average income, and what to do once

According to the Women's Institute for a Secure Retirement, "While the poverty rate for all women age 65 and older is 10.6% (or just over 1 in 10), the poverty rate for single women living alone is almost twice as high at 19%. Older persons living alone are much more likely to be poor (15%) than older persons living with families (6%). The highest poverty rates are experienced among older Hispanic women (41%) who live alone. . . . Unfortunately, older Hispanic and Asian women are the least likely to be kept out of poverty because of Social Security because they are less likely eligible for Social Security income."

you've started maxing out your retirement contributions (which is, in and of itself, a *huge* milestone worth celebrating). Remember that while some aspects of retirement planning can be discouraging if you're not in a place to contribute more or improve upon your strategies immediately, getting in the right mindset to make good decisions for your future as you start to earn more is crucial, and picking up books like this one is a sure sign that you're on the right track. "Through a combination of prioritization, budgeting, skill building, and strategically increasing your income," Amanda said, "you will find the space to save and invest."

LOOKING BEYOND THE BASICS OF RETIREMENT PLANNING WITH AMANDA HOLDEN

Is financial independence possible for people who have an "average" household income?

My most honest answer is that it will be very difficult for a person in an average-income household to reach financial independence, at no fault of their own. Especially without the help of company pensions and potentially Social Security and Medicare. Astronomic growth in the costs of housing, medical care, energy, education, food, and childcare has blown out any chance the U.S. has of maintaining a stable middle class. The best solutions will not be happening in our personal Excel spreadsheets, but on a societal level.

That said, it may be difficult, but not impossible. Would you rather rock up to retirement age with nothing or with something? Don't be intimidated by that big future number or the financial independence bros who are out here cosplaying life on the Oregon Trail; focus on what you can do *now*. Put some real time into learning about investing, as soon as possible! Stop guessing about something as important as your literal financial freedom! Mistakes are absolutely a part of the learning curve, but let's avoid a scenario where you miss out on returns or are paying ridiculous, hidden investment fees because of a lack of education! When you're not already wealthy, there is not as much room for error.

A lot of us know the "expert advice" to put 10 to 15% of our income toward retirement, but how can you tell if your current investment strategy is actually putting you on track toward the future you want?

Across financial planning best practices, 10% to retirement is not generally considered enough. Fifteen percent may not even cover it. That old 10% rule was predicated on a lot of assumptions: a person having a pension, a person being invested correctly for forty years of a career, the market producing historical 10% returns, etc. Hopefully, retirement is the biggest expense of our lifetimes! Hopefully, we do get thirty years of living out our deepest future-self fantasies. But there's no denying that saving and investing for the future is a big job. Think of it this way: You have one income to afford two lifetimes. Knowing this, how much should we save?

Simple answer is: Use a good online calculator! A good one will take into consideration personal details such as taxes, inflation, and Social Security. And that's because there are lots of variables to consider! Therefore, comparing the results from a few of these will give you a good idea about your progress.

How should someone go about tweaking their investment strategy as they get older?

The advice you'll usually hear is to move into a more conservative strategy as you approach and live in retirement. ("Conservative" just means more bonds and cash, and fewer stocks.) When you're young, you can handle more ups and downs, which you do in service of longer-term growth. When you're older and attempting to live off your investments, volatility isn't ideal. This is still a good strategy, but we also have to consider that we are living so much longer than previous generations. Some people reading this will live to be a hundred and ten! So moving into a super-conservative strategy at age sixty-five might actually hurt our chances at making our money last.

I think of it like this: In the years leading up to retirement, I will start to move some of our stock investments into cash and short-term bonds so that I've got five years of living expenses covered. I would only do this in years where the stock market is "positive," taking gains to put into the "holding tank." This way, I don't have to tap into volatile stock investments even if I retire into a bad market. Those investments are allowed to keep working without interruption, growing for years. In years when the market behaves, I will take some profits and refill the tank.

One thing to remember: Robots are already able to plan this transition out for us and that's only going to get better!

Speaking to hourly/tipped/gig workers who are often left out of the investing conversation: Is an IRA going to be enough to retire on? Are there other resources to look into?

IRA contribution limits have nothing to do with how much money you actually need to live in retirement. It's simply how much the IRS allows you to put into one of these accounts. Remember, an IRA is a place where you get a tax incentive if you use it to invest for the long term. But naturally, there are limits to the generosity of the IRS!

A traditional or Roth IRA alone may not be enough to retire on, but it's a fantastic start. If you are religious about maxing out (and actually investing the money in) an IRA every year, you'd be in pretty great shape!

If you've maxed out your IRA and have more to invest, don't stop there! The easiest thing to do is invest in a "regular" investing account, also known as a brokerage account. A regular ol' investing account doesn't get the special tax treatment of an IRA or other retirement account, but it does have total flexibility for use. There are no rules about who can use it or for what purpose. With these accounts, you'll need to report investment gains (like dividends) on your taxes each year, but don't be intimidated! Your bank will provide you with the tax docs you need.

FILL ME IN

Amanda Holden's Guide to Visualizing Your Retirement Needs

Below, Amanda has kindly provided a simplified way to calculate what you'll need in retirement. Remember, there are plenty of online calculators available to you, so I recommend using one of those as well!

Start with how much money you want each year in retirement in "today's dollars." This is called your "replacement rate," or the amount you'll need to replace your salary in retirement:
$________________ / year

Next, you'll want to get a starting estimate for your target retirement number. Get that by multiplying your replacement rate by 25 (this number is going to be large; don't be intimidated out of doing any planning!):
$________________

Why multiply by 25? This is the reverse operation of taking 4% from your portfolio. With the 4% rule, you take 4% off the top of your investment "pile" each year. You are living off the profits of your investments, ideally without digging into the principal; the idea is to keep that principal generating profits for you to live on. So, if you have $1 million total invested, the 4% rule says you can take $40,000 per year from your investments. But it's easier to start with the smaller number, with the amount you'll need each year—your replacement rate. Then, back the truck up: $40,000 multiplied by 25 is $1 million.

FILL ME IN

There are some criticisms of the 4% rule. 1) The actual study, called the Liberty Study, only looked at thirty years of longevity, not perpetuity, and 2) most personal financial planning now assumes that future returns will not be as high as past returns. It is a safer assumption to use 3% or 3.5%, which would mean multiplying by 33.3 and 28.5, respectively.

Next, get comfortable with a compound interest calculator. I like the one provided by the U.S. government at investor.gov. Fill out the online calculator with your information, including the current balance of your investment accounts, your monthly contributions, and your expected rate of investment return. What do you see? How much more would you need to increase your monthly contributions to reach your target number?

____

____

____

____

____

Unfortunately, no one can predict the future here! The U.S. stock market has historically returned an annual average of over 10%. History may repeat itself, but maybe not! I'd personally start by using 6% or 7% annually compounded, which are safer assumptions.

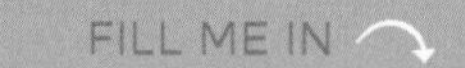

Adjust for income tax. Remember that if you are pulling from a pre-tax/tax-deferred retirement account, you will have to pay income taxes on the dollars you withdraw.
Round up your target contribution by 20% by multiplying it by 1.2:
$____________________

*Round up by *at least* 20%, if not more! Your retirement tax bracket will vary depending on how much you withdraw each year and where you live. Tax brackets may be different from what they are now by the time you retire, but you'll reference the same income tax brackets that you use to determine tax on employment income to determine your retirement taxes.*

Add any other potential sources of income in retirement that will cover some of your annual needs. If you have an ever-elusive pension, that will go here, and some people will consider their expected Social Security payments. Others won't, because these payments are not necessarily guaranteed. List those potential sources here:

____

____

____

____

____

____

____

____

FILL ME IN

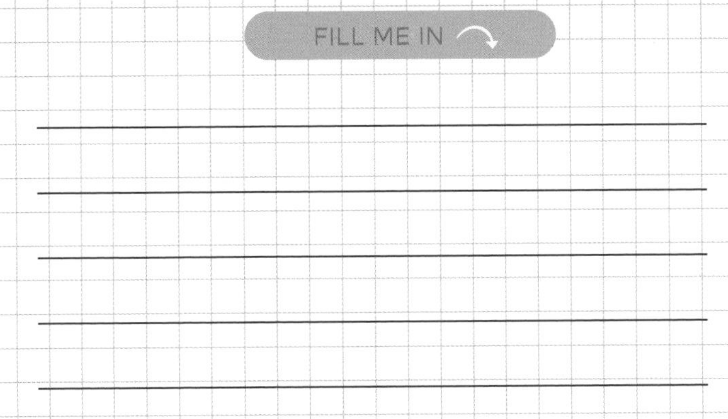

Again, this is purposefully oversimplified to give you a starting framework. Each person should adjust accordingly!

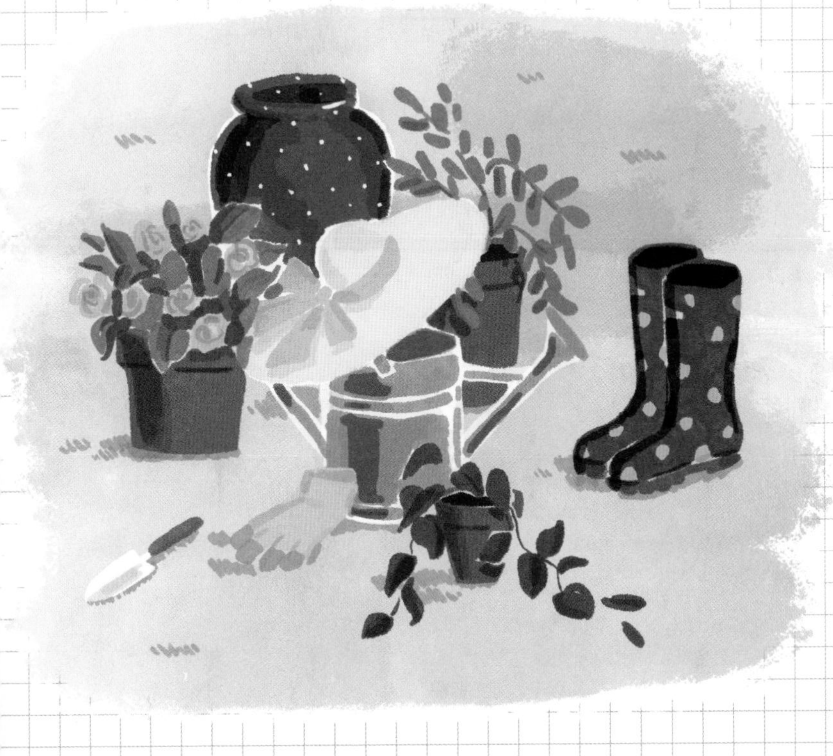

5

STUDENT LOAN RELIEF AND THE LIE OF THE ENTITLED MILLENNIAL

In August of 2022, Peter and I got dressed up, treated ourselves to a cab, and took ourselves to The River Café, quite possibly the fanciest restaurant in all of Brooklyn, where we'd go on to eat the absolute most expensive meal of our lives so far. Even though it technically had a dress code, we both felt overdressed compared to the rest of the clientele. Peter was in a full suit and tie, while the rest of the men seemed at least mildly inconvenienced to have to wear a jacket—after all, dropping $175 per plate (*not* including the $30 cocktails and a list of wines by the bottle that tiptoed well into the four-figure range) was a normal Friday night for them. For us, though, it was a very special occasion. We had finally paid off Peter's student loans and were there to celebrate. (I say "we" because we do share finances, but I should give credit where credit is due. Which is to say, the credit is pretty much his, as he was paying off these loans by himself for the better part of a decade before we got married.)

That same month, President Biden's administration announced it was finally making good on its word and enacting the federal student loan forgiveness program that was a cornerstone of its campaign—or, at least, a semblance of the plan his campaign proposed. More than one person asked if Peter was annoyed by the announcement, since it wouldn't benefit him personally. The truth was that he didn't spend one second resenting the fact that he'd already paid off all his loans, because they were no longer his problem. Would he have been glad to take advantage of the forgiveness program? Absolutely! But he also wouldn't have qualified for it. For one thing, we made too much money, as our household income was in the top 5% of the country, and that was the Biden team's announced cutoff. For another, he had refinanced his loans five years earlier through a private lender, and federal relief only applied to public loans. But most importantly, he didn't care that other, less financially privileged people would benefit from debt relief and not him, because he's not an absolute jackass.

Yet that is what was asked of him, because that's what the media was focusing on. Not "look how many people's lives will be better because of this." Not "look how the government is finally course correcting, since the availability of federal funding has not kept pace with the increasing cost of a higher education." The focus was overwhelmingly on the question, "But is this *fair?*" (Is it fair that average earners must save up for years before going to places like The River Café to celebrate a special occasion, while rich people who couldn't care less go every week to sit at their usual table? No—but nobody cares about "fairness" until the government does something that actually helps the working class.)

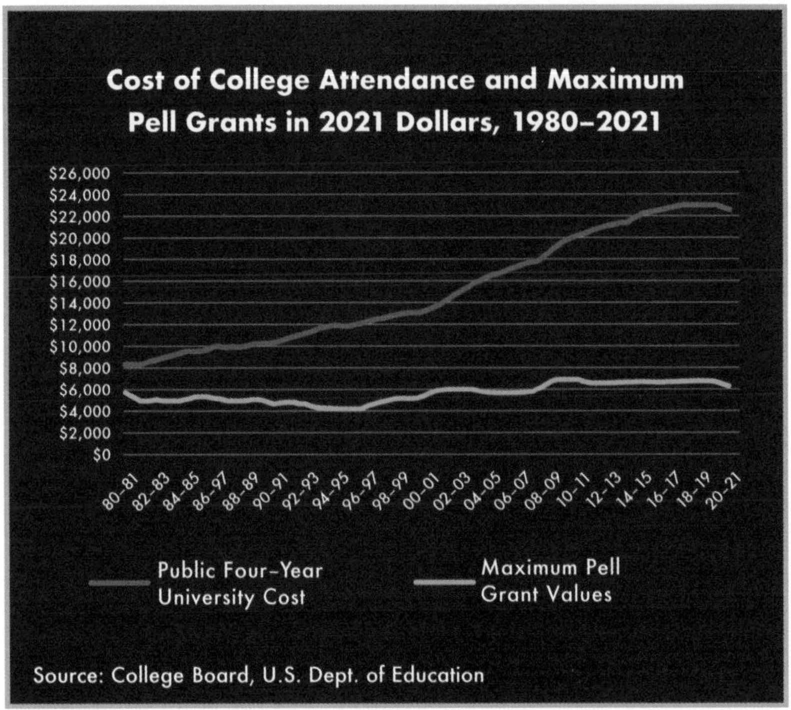

Student Debt Relief Is Not "Millennial Entitlement"

I'm writing this in early March of 2023, and the future in regard to student loan forgiveness is very opaque. The Biden administration's relief plan is currently being reviewed in court thanks to two separate lawsuits being brought against it, and we likely won't know the outcome for months. But even if Biden's student debt relief plan (or some other version of federal student loan relief) has gone through by the time this book is published, there are still millions of Americans who will not have benefited due to having taken out private loans, either initially or through a refinance. Yet when the plan was announced, there was an avalanche of backlash in the mainstream media, especially from center- and right-leaning commentators. Articles with titles like "Opinion: Biden's student loan forgiveness is unfair and unwise" or even "Student loan 'forgiveness' is a liberal sacrifice to millennial resentments," an opinion from the Association of Mature American Citizens, a conservative advocacy group, dismissed the move as simply "buying votes" of people who'd benefit, ignoring the immediate and necessary relief it would provide people facing a financial situation they likely didn't understand they were signing up for. Because when the vast majority of them signed on for their loans, they were children, or just barely past that point.

In order to better comprehend the real-world impact of Biden's student debt relief plan, I spoke with Cindy Zuniga-Sanchez, founder of Zero-Based Budget Coaching LLC, whom we've been collaborating with for years now at TFD. Having paid off over $200,000 in loans herself, Cindy is a student debt expert. She also happens to be a former commercial litigation attorney, a career she took a break from when she was financially stable enough to take her personal finance business full-time. When I asked about the potential impact of President Biden's student debt relief plan, she was quick to point out that forty million

Millennial (n.):
a catchall term referring to any young person who comes across as entitled for simply asking for the same social safety nets and privileges that were afforded to previous generations; often used to convey a condescending perception of childishness despite the fact that these individuals are fully grown adults

borrowers would see their loan balance decrease—90% of whom are earning less than $75,000. "Notably, this targeted relief will help advance racial equity by benefiting Pell Grant recipients, which are significantly comprised of Black and Hispanic/Latino students," Cindy said. "Student loan forgiveness is critical to minimizing the racial wealth gap and advancing economic mobility. If the Supreme Court strikes down the program, millions of Americans—many of whom faced disproportionate economic hardship during the COVID-19 global pandemic—will have to reprioritize their financial goals and, unfortunately, potentially struggle with debt repayment."

The fact is, this generation is facing an unprecedented crisis when it comes to finances, and student loans are just one piece of the puzzle. I've already mentioned the fact that as of this writing, the federal minimum wage hasn't been raised in over sixteen years. In real-life terms, that stagnation is even more stark; when adjusted for inflation, today's federal minimum wage is 40% *less* than the minimum wage in 1970. And again adjusting for inflation, the average cost of college tuition has increased 747.8% since 1963. No, that's not a typo. Tuition is now *over 700%* what it was in the 1960s. Yet many of us grew up with the message that college was a nonnegotiable, or our only chance at a better life than our parents had.

It's incredibly frustrating to hear baby boomers complain about millennial entitlement when millennials (and Gen-Xers and Gen-Zers) are dealing with the fallout of policies and government programs that were literally stripped *because* of the boomer generation. In her book *Can't Even: How Millennials Became the Burnout Generation*, journalist Anne Helen Petersen reminds us that boomers and their parents "helped elect leaders like President Ronald Reagan, who promised to 'protect' the middle class through tax cuts, even though Reagan's policies, once put in practice, worked to defund many of the programs that had allowed the middle class to achieve that status in the first place."

This is not to say that *all* people from previous generations have benefited from government programs and funding that is unfathomable at the same level for millennials. The G.I. Bill, for instance, provided funds for attending college and buying homes to millions of soldiers returning home from World War II, but was designed to largely exclude Black veterans. And poverty and financial hardship are generational; with student debt in particular, Black borrowers have been hit the hardest. As journalist Erin Blakemore wrote for *History*, "twenty years after first enrolling in school, the typical Black borrower who started college in the 1995–96 school year still owed 95% of their original student debt."

Cindy Zuniga-Sanchez also provided a general look at how the student loan crisis is affecting marginalized groups, and how it particularly affects non-white women: "Black women are paid $0.57, Native women $0.50, and Hispanic/Latina women $0.49 for every dollar paid to a white, non-Hispanic/Latino man. Because women from marginalized communities are less likely to benefit from generational wealth or a college fund (e.g., a 529 plan), they are more likely to take on student loans."

As a result of those cuts and policies, we now have rising living costs, depressed wages, a higher cost to obtain a higher education to even get a "good" job in the first place, and way fewer unions to protect us once we are there. We have threadbare remnants of the social safety net that was put in place for the middle class in the postwar period, and not enough leaders who are willing to do something about it. On top of that, we have boomers telling us we should just be grateful, and that if we want to change our situation, it's completely within our own individual power. "The myth of the wholly self-made American," Petersen writes, "like all myths, relies on some sort of sustained willful ignorance—often perpetuated by those who've already benefited from them." Of course millennials are resentful; who wouldn't be?

"Okay, but I Still Have Student Loans"

Unfortunately, I'm not harping on the impossible situation millennials have been placed in because I have an answer. I personally believe Biden's proposed student debt relief plan is a step in the right direction, but time will tell how it pans out—and there is still a lot more that needs to change. What I *am* aiming to do here is remind you that, if you are one of the millions of Americans struggling with student loan debt, it is not your fault. And you still deserve to better your situation, whether you will benefit from much-deserved debt relief or not. But like many financial situations, the answer to what you should do about your own student debt is both simple and not: It depends.

One of the key things to remember is that any future legislation will likely apply to federal student loans, not private loans. Refinancing is a tool that many turn to to get their debt under control, and it can be a great option. If you already have private student loans, it often makes complete sense to refinance to get a better payoff situation for yourself. However, if you currently have only federal student loans in your name, it might make more sense to hold on to them.

What is student loan refinancing?
Basically, refinancing your loans means you make an agreement with a private lender wherein they will pay off all your debt for you and replace it with one new loan, which you then pay off through them directly. You can refinance with different goals in mind, too, either to lower your current monthly payment obligation, or to get a lower interest rate, which can help you pay less toward your loans in the long run.

Let's use my personal life (my husband's, really) as an example. Peter refinanced his loans five years ago, putting himself on a plan that effectively cut his repayment timeline in half. This meant he would save money in the long run, because he got a lower interest rate, which lowered the total amount he would pay over time. And, like I mentioned, he wouldn't have qualified for student debt relief due to our household income, so it's not as if he wishes he'd done anything differently in hindsight. However, if we were at a lower income and had refinanced those loans, we wouldn't have been able to take advantage of debt relief options we'd have otherwise qualified for.

Running the Refinancing Numbers

For more literal math, let's look at two instances of choosing to refinance your student loans:

If you want to pay off your loans more quickly:

> Say you owe $20,000 in private student loans, with an interest rate of 7%, a monthly payment of $340—you will pay off your loans in about six years. You could pay off your loans more quickly with a higher monthly payment and a lower interest rate. For example, if you refinance to a loan with a 5% interest rate and pay $460 a month, you'll pay $120 more a month than your original amount—but you would pay it off two years earlier and save a total of $2,456 in the long run.

If you want to lower your monthly payment:

> On the other hand, you may want to refinance because your current monthly payment is too difficult to fit in your budget. Using the original amount from the above example, say you refinance to a loan with a 4.5% interest rate and a ten-year term. Your new monthly payment would be $200, freeing up $140 in your budget. You may not save *much* more in the long run (about $180 total), but if you have a tight budget, that extra wiggle room each month could go a long way.

Also, this decision stuck him with a whopping $850 monthly payment for five years. We luckily didn't face any major financial hardship during that time, and if we had, he likely would have been able to refinance again to get a lower monthly payment. His main objective, though, was to prioritize paying off his debt. Would I have made the same decision by myself? Likely not, because no matter what the timeline was, $850 was a tremendous chunk of our monthly budget, and if the post-COVID years have taught me anything, it's the importance of available liquid cash. But was it also nice to suddenly have that money freed up in the budget when we *did* finally pay his loans off? Begrudgingly, I'll say yes.

The point is, student loan repayment is a personal decision. Sometimes it does make sense to pay off your loans as quickly as possible, but sometimes it doesn't. And again, there are people out there who are better equipped to speak to this issue than I am. To that end, I asked Cindy to answer several more questions on the future of student loans and how to judge what the best path is for your personal situation.

THE FUTURE OF STUDENT LOANS WITH CINDY ZUNIGA-SANCHEZ

What do you think the future of college education/ student loans looks like? What do you hope it looks like, and is that hope realistic?

Unless the government passes targeted measures, the cost of a college education will continue to disproportionately rise (in comparison to the relative inflation) and student loan balances will continue to increase. My hope is that the government will enact bipartisan measures to address the price tag of higher education and the growing student debt.

The Biden administration has taken steps in the right direction, including increasing the maximum Pell Grant, providing billions to colleges and universities under the American Rescue Plan, increasing and improving the approval process for loan forgiveness programs including Public Service Loan Forgiveness, and proposing making student loan payments more manageable for both current and future borrowers by capping payments to no more than 5% of a borrower's discretionary income on undergraduate loans and covering the borrower's unpaid monthly interest. We need to continue applying pressure on our elected officials to support and expand these measures.

What general course of action do you recommend for people who have federal student loans, specifically with regard to potential legislation?

Borrowers with federal student loans should familiarize themselves with their repayment options. For example, Income-Driven Repayment (IDR) plans base their monthly payments on the borrower's reported income and are generally lower than payments under the Standard Repayment Plan. Borrowers should also explore whether they are eligible for forgiveness programs such as Public Service Loan Forgiveness, which discharges student loan balances for workers in the public sector upon meeting certain requirements. Borrowers may also explore deferment and forbearance options, which temporarily postpone or reduce student loan payments. For complete details on the various repayment options, loan forgiveness programs, forbearance, and deferment, visit studentaid.gov.

What general course of action do you recommend for private student loans?

Because borrowers with private student loans are generally ineligible for relief that the government offers to those with federal student loans, they should first consult with their lender on any borrower assistance options. Borrowers might also explore refinancing their student loans, which may lower their interest rates and, in some cases, even shorten their repayment periods.

Borrowers should also look into alternative forgiveness options, such as state-sponsored loan forgiveness programs (e.g., NYS Teacher Loan Forgiveness Program), as well as student loan repayment programs or benefits that their employers may offer.

Is there any instance where paying off student debt as quickly as possible may not be the best choice? Why or why not?

There are certainly instances where paying off student debt as quickly as possible may not be the best choice. For example, if your student debt carries a low interest rate—say, less than 7%—you may be better off directing money that you would have used to make an additional payment to your student debt to the stock market instead (since the stock market has a historical rate of return of 10%). By investing early, you allow time and compound interest to work their magic by growing your money for your future self. With that said, there honestly is no right or wrong strategy. Choosing how you will prioritize your debt repayment and other money goals is highly personal to your goals and comfort level.

FILL ME IN

Flowchart: Choosing the Best Debt Payoff Plan for You

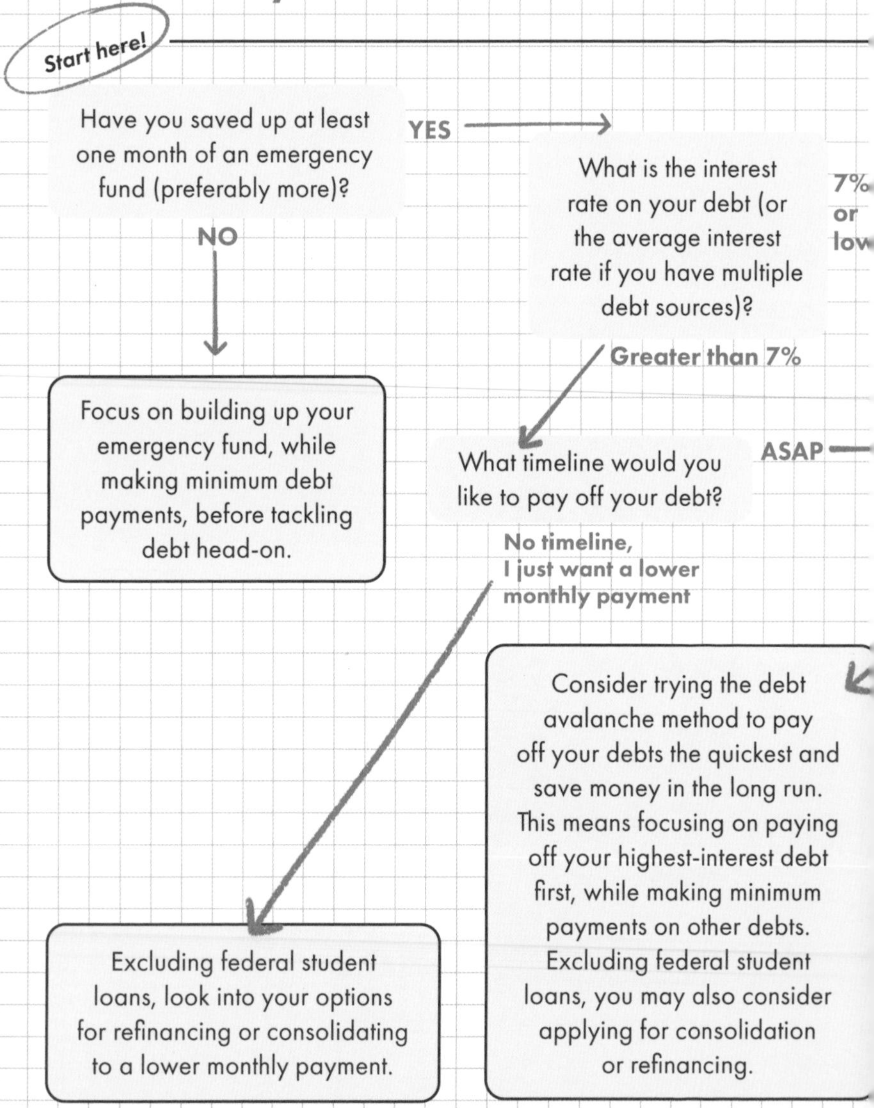

Start here!

Have you saved up at least one month of an emergency fund (preferably more)?

YES →

What is the interest rate on your debt (or the average interest rate if you have multiple debt sources)?

7% or low

Greater than 7%

What timeline would you like to pay off your debt?

ASAP —

No timeline, I just want a lower monthly payment

NO

Focus on building up your emergency fund, while making minimum debt payments, before tackling debt head-on.

Consider trying the debt avalanche method to pay off your debts the quickest and save money in the long run. This means focusing on paying off your highest-interest debt first, while making minimum payments on other debts. Excluding federal student loans, you may also consider applying for consolidation or refinancing.

Excluding federal student loans, look into your options for refinancing or consolidating to a lower monthly payment.

FILL ME IN

Whether you have student loans or other debt (even credit card debt), you're always going to have an internal debate: *Should I pay this off as quickly as possible? Or should I just coast making the minimum payments?* Use the flowchart below to determine an optimal debt payoff plan for your situation.

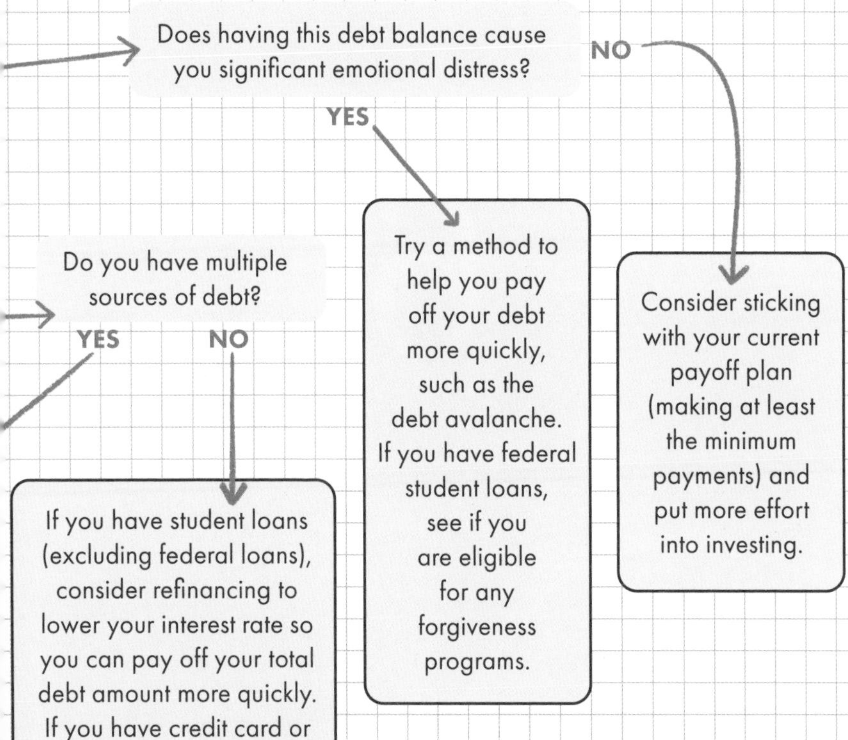

Does having this debt balance cause you significant emotional distress?

YES → Try a method to help you pay off your debt more quickly, such as the debt avalanche. If you have federal student loans, see if you are eligible for any forgiveness programs.

NO → Consider sticking with your current payoff plan (making at least the minimum payments) and put more effort into investing.

Do you have multiple sources of debt?

YES

NO → If you have student loans (excluding federal loans), consider refinancing to lower your interest rate so you can pay off your total debt amount more quickly. If you have credit card or consumer debt, a balance transfer card with a 0% APR period—just make sure you can pay off the full amount before the real APR kicks in!

Reminder: To ensure you are approved and getting the best interest rate possible, you will want to make sure your credit is in tip-top shape before applying for debt consolidation, refinancing, or a balance-transfer credit card.

6

HOW TO END YOUR "BEING CHEAP" ERA FOR GOOD

As I investigated earlier in this book, avoiding lifestyle inflation necessitates cutting back on spending that's not serving you—but that doesn't mean it's a reason to spend as little as possible. Unfortunately, we live in an era of cheapness. Not frugality, but *cheapness*.

It's impossible to navigate the world of money advice without stumbling upon list after list after list of hacks for spending as little money as possible. Sometimes the advice is harmless, or even helpful, with TikToks promising dupes for everything from re-creating your favorite overpriced Sweetgreen salad at home to mimicking the look of a built-in bookcase with an IKEA shelving unit. Certainly, easy access to advice for making your life less expensive can be a good thing, especially for those who have little disposable income. But other times, the advice to spend cheaply is actually encouraging us to spend *more*, and more mindlessly, often at the cost of things like the environment or the labor value of people we'll never meet. And there is perhaps no worse a perpetuator of encouraging mindless spending than Shein.

Shein and the Normalization of Cheap

Fast fashion isn't anything new. The term has been thrown around since at least the late nineties, when companies like Zara, Forever 21, and H&M started taking over the American retail market, offering more style options for less money. Online shopping also made us get used to the idea that getting a new outfit is simply a matter of clicking a few buttons. Fast fashion was already eroding the environment and our connections with both the places our clothes were coming from and the people

Fast Fashion (n.):
a large subset of the fashion industry that tricks you into thinking you're saving money with the drastically cheap price of individual items—subsequently encouraging you to increase the total number of items you "add to cart"

who were making them. Then Shein saw what those brands were doing and said, *Hold my beer.*

Whereas high-end designers release collections seasonally, fast-fashion brands typically operate on a fifty-two-week cycle—each week is a new season, rather than each quarter. But Shein, an online-only retailer based in China, doesn't just list new clothing items on a weekly basis: According to *The Guardian*, as of April 2022, they were estimated to be listing up to 10,000 new items *per day*, having surpassed Amazon as the most-downloaded shopping app in 2021.

While other fast-fashion brands need about a month to get clothes from the design phase to the ready-to-sell stage, Shein only needs a week. In the media, they've been called "real-time retail," illustrating how the company has mastered the ever-changing demand from a thirsty consumer base tuned in to TikTok haul videos 24/7. And the impact of this incredible output is exactly what you would expect. Shein's labor practices are an ongoing nightmare, with Swiss watchdog Public Eye revealing that several of their manufacturers were unofficial factories set up in residential buildings, some with no emergency exits and barred windows—conditions in breach of Chinese labor laws. A separate investigation from U.K. broadcaster Channel 4 found that Shein was being supplied by factories with employees working up to eighteen hours a day for as little as 4¢ per item. And while the fast-fashion industry is responsible for an estimated 10% of global carbon emissions, Shein alone makes up 28% of the fast-fashion market in the U.S.

The objective badness of fast fashion is common knowledge now. So why do companies like Shein still have such massive appeal? When you spend even a minute perusing the website, it becomes crystal clear: It is profoundly, absurdly cheap. Click on the "tops" section, for instance, and you'll see dozens of options on the first page of offerings for only $5.

That said, this is not to shame anyone for shopping at these brands: For many people, fast fashion may be all they can afford. Someone with only $50 to spend on new work clothes may only be able to find a blouse

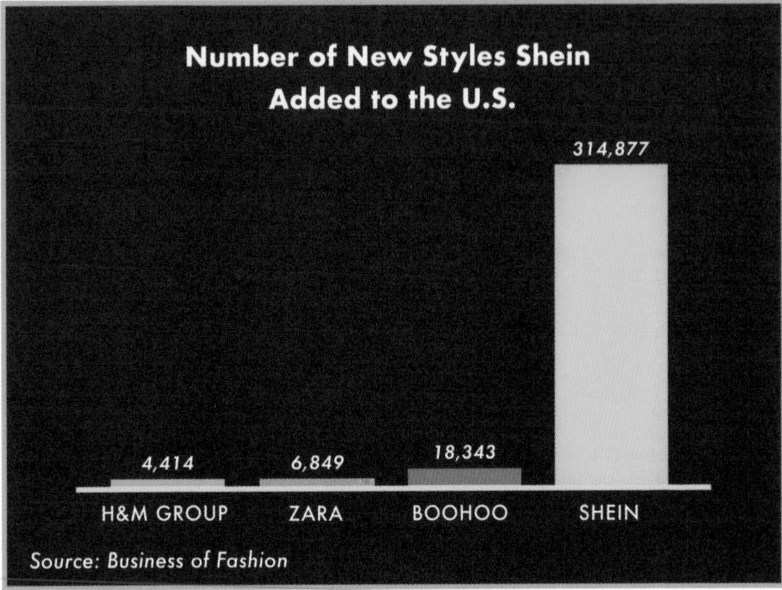

or a pair of pants elsewhere but be able to get several outfit options from Shein for the same cost. Also, compared with many other retailers, fast-fashion companies tend to offer wider ranges of clothing for people who are plus-sized. But for many, the allure is simply that they can buy as much as they want without spending nearly what they would at other stores. Search #sheinhaul on TikTok and you'll find endless videos showing off hauls of $100, $200, even $500 spent on Shein. I'm sorry, but anyone who can afford to spend $500 on outfits that will fall apart after three laundry cycles can also afford to upgrade to brands with clothes made to last.

There's no doubt that having access to necessities like affordable clothing should be a human right; however, the existence of companies like Shein perpetuates the myth that minimum wage is a livable wage, because *look, you can buy a shirt for just $5*! But our consumerist addiction to constantly acquire more is the real issue here. And that's the worst thing that making faster and cheaper fashion has done: encourage us to believe that we *deserve* to buy as much as possible for as little as possible. When we get accustomed to spending the bare minimum on things like clothing, anything that costs more is going to seem like a rip-off. We then believe our consumer habits are worth exploiting impoverished factory workers and the environment over, either because that exploitation is invisible to us or because we just accept it as a fact of life.

Of course, social media is also to blame here. When we see celebrities, influencers, even our own friends, showing off new outfits at every wedding, night out, or party, we feel desensitized to the dopamine hit of adding just one or two well-fitting items to our wardrobe. If we can access an excessive number of options to the point that so much choice feels normal, even mundane, we are inevitably going to feel increasingly dissatisfied with what we already have. At the same time, we feel entitled to those shockingly low prices. And this constant desire to obtain more while paying less doesn't just cheapen us financially—it cheapens us spiritually, and it erodes our sense of value about everything, including ourselves and our relationships.

An Abundance Mindset, Not an Excess Mindset

Security is a financial characteristic, but it's also a philosophical one. A secure person knows that if she gets an unexpected parking ticket, she can afford to pay it off without letting it take up any more space in her thoughts than necessary. She feels comfortable and excited to spend on hostess gifts or treat a friend to dinner on occasion, because those things aren't going to make a difference in her bottom line. A secure person also feels confident in what she already has and knows that spending money on a flashy vacation or a hundred Shein outfits isn't going to magically turn her into a different, better version of herself.

Security is *truly* aspirational, because it means you can part with your money when you want to or need to, but don't feel influenced to buy things you don't actually need, or even want. And in order to feel free from the urge to always spend money, you must learn the difference between an "abundance mindset" and an "excess mindset."

Having an abundance mindset means you're not scared to spend more, because you know there's enough to go around. Traditionally, the opposite of an abundance mindset is a scarcity mindset; this is the feeling that money and resources are limited, so you need to take what's available as soon as you can. For financial therapist Lindsay Bryan-Podvin, the key to financial balance means existing somewhere between scarcity and excess:

> **"I use a 'both/and' approach with my clients to help them rewrite their money stories in a neutral or positive way, without negating their real challenges. This means honoring their struggles while striving for a new financial behavior or viewpoint. Holding space for two things at once comes from many different philosophical viewpoints, but it is often used in DBT, or Dialectical Behavioral Therapy.**
>
> **"For money, the both/and might look like combining two truths that seem to be in opposition. Such as 'I want to travel more this year' and 'I want to pay down my credit cards.' Instead of either/or, a both/and solution could be 'I'm going to focus on paying down my credit cards, and to ensure I have my traveling needs met, I'll do a house swap with a friend who lives in a city I've been wanting to visit.' (A shame-only approach might say this person doesn't deserve to travel until they are debt free.)"**

Unfortunately, the idea of an abundance mindset can get oversimplified, especially as it has been popularized by fearmongering gurus like Tony Robbins and, perhaps more relevant to women in our age group, Rachel Hollis. These people make millions of dollars selling life coaching services and tickets to "motivational speaking" conferences hawking empty promises of success if you simply do what they tell you. They don't allow room for nuance, leaving followers to believe that an abundance mindset means always saying yes, damn the costs or consequences. But I would argue this is an excess mindset, not an abundance mindset.

Living abundantly, instead of excessively, means understanding when you have enough. This is where a lot of people find themselves in trouble when trying to move beyond the just-getting-by stage of their finances. For many of us, having more to spend in a month can be such a profound life change that it's easy to go overboard and give in to lifestyle inflation ("inflating your ego," but also your id, if you're thinking in shame-free budgeting terms). But buying more, like the influencers showing off their $500 Shein hauls, just because you *technically can*, isn't living abundantly. It is living excessively, and is the definition of FOMO. And that is just another side of the same coin of living scarcely: living in fear that there isn't enough money, time, resources, or experiences to go around, so you must jump on opportunities as soon as you can.

Also, having more clothes than you even realistically have time to wear could mean you're creating a bigger issue for yourself. At one point, style influencer Christina Mychas ended up getting rid of 60% of her closet, because she realized that buying whatever she wanted was making her *less* happy with what she owned.

> **"I realized that the more I added to my wardrobe, and the more I pursued the idea of wearing something different every day, the more confused I felt about my own style. It gets to the place where you don't feel comfortable in what you're wearing, and the clothes start wearing you, instead of you wearing the clothes. I found that, actually, the more I repeated outfits, the more I found a style foundation. I don't wear the same thing every day, but I wear a variation of it—I love a blazer, a top, and a pair of pants. I started wearing that formula a lot, and that's when I started to feel most like myself."**

How to Stop Living Cheaply Without Going Broke

The popularity of Shein is just one example of how we've grown accustomed to overconsuming. Another is our relationship to sales. A scarcity mindset is seeing that Anthropologie is having a huge sale and spending hundreds of dollars on twee home decor items, because you'll never get deals this good again. Only later will you realize you don't *love* everything you got, but you're stuck with it because everything was final sale.

Conversely, having an abundance mindset means planning ahead (perhaps with one of your "sinking funds"—don't worry, we'll get to those later in this chapter) so you can take your time searching for the perfect rug or floor lamp and buying it as soon as you come across it, because you know it is well within your means. But in order to get to that level, we need to have a better understanding of what sales actually are—and how they often work against us. Advertisers know that many of us default to a scarcity mindset and use that to their advantage. Sales say "Today only!" to make you think that you have to act quickly in order to save money, even though that's not the case. And this has become even more intense in the era of creepily targeted ads on social media.

To be transparent, it's not like TFD hasn't used sales to promote our products, and I would never begrudge companies (especially ethical and independently owned ones) for doing what they have to do. It just means that, as the consumer, you must know the difference between when you really, truly want something, and when you're just feeling FOMO. Thinking abundantly means understanding that if you don't get this one handbag, there will be other handbags in the future. It is the opposite of FOMO.

Reminder:
Retailers do not have sales in order to save *you* money. They have them so *they* can earn more, because the more items they sell, even at a discount, the more revenue they're going to generate overall. A $100 pair of jeans at 40% off isn't saving you $40; you're still spending $60 you may not have necessarily spent.

FILL ME IN

Reflection Activity: Curing Your Spending FOMO

Use the space below to reflect on purchases you've made based on a scarcity or excess mindset, and which have actually added value to your life. To start, take a walk through your home, or sift through your closet. What items can you point to that were either lackluster or thoughtful choices?

Mindless Purchases You Regret

Intentional Purchases You'd Happily Buy Again

FILL ME IN

Visualization: The Abundant Living Matrix

Use the matrix here to plot out your material, social, and interpersonal spending behaviors, and refer to it when reassessing your spending. Remember that the best options will always fall on the "intentional" half of the matrix but may be either "frugal" or "lavish"—spending intentionally *can* mean spending more, but it won't always. Here's an example of how I would plot certain spending decisions when deciding where to get a new couch:

- Frugal & Mindless: Buying a low-quality futon from a big-box store
- Frugal & Intentional: Spending hours searching until you find the perfect secondhand option on Facebook Marketplace
- Lavish & Mindless: Putting a high-end couch on a credit card before you can afford it
- Lavish & Intentional: Contributing to a new-couch sinking fund and buying the best option for your home when you can afford it

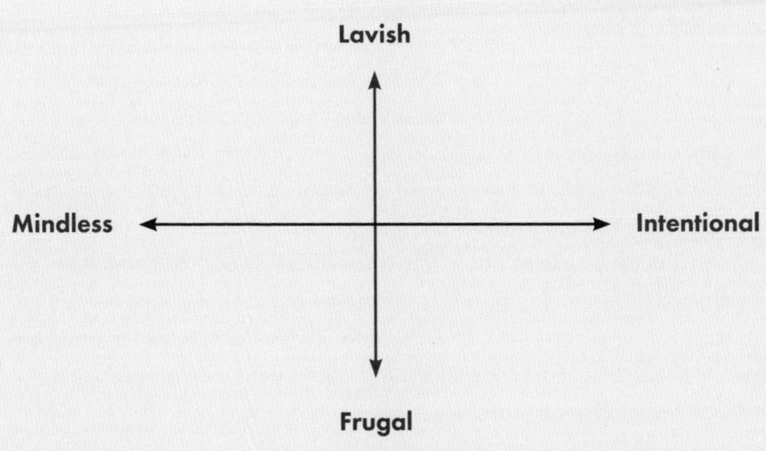

An abundance mindset is also important in other aspects of your finances, like investing. If you're thinking in terms of scarcity, you're more likely to make hasty, emotional decisions, such as selling off stocks when there's a downturn in the market. This may ultimately end up costing you, because historically, the market has always recovered. Selling off assets means missing out on huge future passive earnings, especially considering the S&P 500 has seen gains of 166% since 2000. An abundance mindset means staying the course with your investments, knowing they will pay off in the future. It means knowing you don't need to make rash decisions today that could negatively impact your future self.

When you're just scraping by, frugality is a necessity. Splitting bills down to the penny, shopping at fast-fashion stores, DIYing old furniture makeovers, sharing streaming passwords—all are totally valid spending decisions when you're barely making ends meet, and even sometimes when you've moved up the financial ladder (though even if you're on a strict budget, there *are* alternatives to shopping fast fashion, like thrifting). Our cultural normalization of cheapness, however, makes it difficult to determine what's worth spending money on and what isn't.

While reading through the different types of cheapness that follow, ask yourself: *Are my own cheap habits sabotaging my happiness?*

Material Cheapness

By now, you can probably identify material cheapness, especially when it comes to fast-fashion brands like Shein. Material cheapness can apply to anything physical you buy, from clothing to furniture and decor to kitchen items to beauty and personal care. It doesn't necessarily mean only buying items at rock-bottom prices, but it does mean valuing a low cost at the expense of an item's quality and your own values as a consumer. Transitioning to a less-but-better mindset, though, is easier said than done. Luckily, you *don't* have to buy the most expensive option possible in order to start consuming less cheaply. Christina Mychas weighs each spending decision carefully, taking into account how an item will actually fit into her overall wardrobe, where it's coming from, and its overall quality:

> **"I like to research things like fabric and composition, but it's also aesthetic. Do you want something that's really classic? Or do you want something more modern and oversized, or totally out there? Look into the ethics of the brand, especially if it's something more expensive—you want your money to go to support something that aligns with what you value. I also look at clothing care. If it's something that is really fussy to take care of, am I even going to wear it? Do I have the money to invest in taking care of it? There are some hidden costs that come with certain garments of clothing, not just what you pay for them up front."**

Transactional Cheapness

A lot of my career has been plagued by hearing about professionals like Tim Ferriss hacking their work lives by outsourcing everything, often by paying an overseas virtual assistant as little as possible to do their work for them. Outsourcing can be a useful tool in making your life easier, but is it worth the cost of knowing you're exploiting someone in a more vulnerable position? That's transactional cheapness, and it refers to cheapness regarding paying other people for their services.

A particularly toxic strain of transactional cheapness is thinking you're entitled to opt out of tipping. Several years ago, there was a small uproar in the personal finance community when an article was published on CNBC's website encouraging people to start tipping 18% instead of 20% in order to save around $400 a year (based on the average person's restaurant spending, I guess). The Ramsey acolytes were beside themselves, saying 18% was already too big of a tip, while more progressive personal finance folks were outraged that a respected news source would encourage a money-saving tip that a) wouldn't necessarily save *all* that much, especially when most of us wouldn't actively go transfer that $3 we "saved" to our savings account each time we went out to eat, and b) would only save someone money by being less fair to others.

The federal minimum wage for tipped workers is only $2.13, and any employee can count as a "tipped worker" if they make a minimum of $30 a month in tips.

No matter how you feel about tipping wages and whether you think the livelihood of tipped workers should be left up to the customer (it shouldn't), the reality is that in most places in America, service workers' livelihoods *are* completely reliant on tips. That doesn't mean it's fair, but not tipping your server isn't making a statement about the quality of your food or restaurant experience. It is communicating to that server, "I don't think you deserve to pay your bills." They say the fastest way to gauge whether your date is a jerk is to pay attention to how they treat restaurant workers, and they are right. Sure, someone can be completely polite to a server and a complete asshole to their loved ones. But have you ever met someone who is always an asshole to servers, but wonderful to everyone they know personally? I didn't think so.

Social Cheapness

This might be the most controversial type of cheapness, but it's an important one to talk about. In tough financial times, splitting bills down to who ate how much of which appetizer can be necessary, and I don't think it's inherently wrong to do so. But when you start earning more, and life becomes more affordable, the splitting-everything mentality can be toxic.

I'm not necessarily talking about always splitting the bill 50/50. When you are doing well financially, it *does* make sense to split 50/50 when the difference between bills would be within a few dollars, or maybe even with a bigger gap. Of course, it can be frustrating to split evenly at a group dinner when you only ate your entree and drank a club soda while everyone else dove into the appetizers and got multiple alcoholic drinks. But in those cases when it really doesn't feel fair to split evenly, I suggest offering to be the person who figures out what everyone owes (apps like Splitwise can make this super simple).

Real social cheapness, however, comes from viewing everything as a transaction. If you treat a friend to brunch or drinks, it shouldn't come with the expectation that they will treat you to the next outing at an exact equivalent value. Maybe being the one who treats isn't something they can afford right now, and who-treats-whom shouldn't be a measurement of whether a friendship is a good one. There should be a natural push and pull to a relationship if everyone is living abundantly. If you do notice that you're the only one who ever offers to pick up the bill, perhaps it's time to assess why you're always offering. Do you genuinely get joy from picking up the tab when you know you can afford it? Or do you do it because you feel like you want to have leverage in the relationship?

On the contrary, if you're someone who never offers to pick up a bill, and who, when not being treated, insists on splitting everything down to the penny, ask yourself if it's worth it. Is it coming from a genuine need to save money, or an obsession? Do you find yourself being invited out less? Do you feel anxious about the idea of paying more than your "fair share," even when the difference you'd end up saving is negligible? If, after some real soul-searching, you find yourself regularly taking the generosity of others for granted, maybe it's time to reevaluate your social spending habits.

Relationship Cheapness

Finally, perhaps the most insidious form of cheapness is being cheap within your romantic relationship. Now, what's "fair" in a relationship isn't necessarily 50/50, especially when it comes to dating. If your partner out-earns you (or vice versa) and you keep your finances separate, there's no reason you should pay the same proportion of your rent. What's even worse, though, is romantic partners who try to make things "equal" by dividing up other household contributions based on who contributes more financially.

For years at TFD, back when we were publishing on our flagship blog, we would regularly receive comments and submissions from women in their twenties who felt okay that they were making less than their boyfriends, because they made up for the difference by contributing to the home they shared in other ways—usually, that meant they did most of the housework. I'm sorry, but any random finance bro hasn't earned the right to treat his girlfriend like a live-in maid simply because he happened to have a foot in the door in an industry that paid him six figures right out of college, and she didn't.

Of course, this kind of cheapness may not be limited to couples in heterosexual relationships, and being a toxic breadwinner isn't inherent to men (nor do all men act like this). But the existing, socially accepted gender dynamics of hetero couples set a precedent to be wary of. Later I'll get into inequities in romantic relationships and households, but if the above sounds like the person you're dating or married to, that's some good evidence that he's a cheap asshole who needs to make some changes.

Sinking Funds: The Best Tool for Living Abundantly

Realistically, spending cheaply can be a difficult habit to break. The thing that helps the most is learning how to plan ahead—even when you don't know what you're planning for.

Picture this scenario: Your best friend announces she's breaking up with her fiancé of four years. You run to her side armed with wine, her favorite Korean fried chicken, and Haribo gummies, secretly thrilled but biting back your I-told-you-so's, even though all your other friends agreed he sucked. You decide she really needs a girls' spa weekend away to take her mind off her ex's toxic voice notes and figuring out where the hell she's going to live. The only problem is that you meticulously planned out your vacation spending at the beginning of the year and didn't account for any wiggle room. Should you cancel your annual leaf-peeping trip to Vermont so you can make it work?

If thinking in terms of your financial ego, superego, and id is a way to budget so you don't really have to budget, sinking funds are your way to plan so you don't have to plan. A "sinking fund" is essentially a revolving savings account; it's money you're regularly setting aside for a specific, ongoing purpose, and you can pull from the fund to spend on said purpose whenever you need to, as long as you have enough money in the account. Sinking funds work best when you automate regular deposits to them, so they are constantly being replenished. (Case in point: Peter and I save about 10% of our take-home pay for vacations and family-related travel, because it's really important to us. Someone recently asked me how we are able to save that much, and it's simple: I have direct deposit set up to put a portion of each paycheck into our travel sinking fund, which I keep in a high-yield savings account, so we never "see" that money as available for our day-to-day spending.)

So, using the girls' weekend example, if you had a sinking fund set up specifically for vacations, you could have just pulled from it to cover this unexpected expense. Automating deposits to various sinking funds means you can simply refer to them whenever you want or need to spend on something.

FILL ME IN

Establishing Your Sinking Funds

Once you've defined your budget parameters, setting up sinking funds is a great way to create a system so you're always prepared for ongoing spending. You can have your sinking fund deposits go directly into your savings from your paycheck so it's separate from your day-to-day spending.

First, list which sinking funds you want to set up.

What are the ongoing expenses you wish you felt more prepared for? You can have as few or as many as you want!

(Examples: vacations, car maintenance, co-pays and regular medical bills, rainy day family fun, annual fees and premiums, holiday spending, etc.)

- ______________________________
- ______________________________
- ______________________________
- ______________________________
- ______________________________

Next, determine how much you want to save in each fund every month.

To calculate a good amount to save each month, look back at last year's spending. How much did you spend on each category in a year? Do you anticipate needing to spend more in the coming months? (E.g., if you have a big trip coming up, you may want to save more in your vacations bucket than you did last year.)

FILL ME IN

Sinking Fund #1:

____

Amount spent annually:

$______________________________

+ Additional cushion:

$______________________________

÷12

= Amount to save monthly:

$______________________________

Sinking Fund #2:

____

Amount spent annually:

$______________________________

+ Additional cushion:

$______________________________

÷12

= Amount to save monthly:

$______________________________

Sinking Fund #3:

____

Amount spent annually:

$______________________________

+ Additional cushion:

$______________________________

÷12

= Amount to save monthly:

$______________________________

Sinking Fund #4:

____

Amount spent annually:

$______________________________

+ Additional cushion:

$______________________________

÷12

= Amount to save monthly:

$______________________________

Sinking Fund #5:

____

Amount spent annually:

$______________________________

+ Additional cushion:

$______________________________

÷12

= Amount to save monthly:

$______________________________

FILL ME IN

Lastly, automate savings to each sinking fund.

You'll want to keep these funds in a high-yield savings account so that you're always earning interest on what you save. If you keep these funds in a checking account, I can basically guarantee you're missing out on free money—not chic! Many online savings accounts these days allow you to divide the money in your account into different categories or savings buckets, so there's no need to set up different savings accounts for each sinking fund, which sounds honestly way too complicated. (Ally Bank first comes to mind as a savings account that features buckets, but they're certainly not paying me to write this, so use whichever provider feels best for you—Betterment, Capital One, Wealthfront, and SmartyPig all have similar functions.)

The easiest way to automate your sinking fund transfers is to set up direct deposits through your payroll provider. Determine how much you want to save in your sinking funds in total each month, and through your savings account, you should be able to automate sorting that into your various individual funds.

If you're paid monthly:

Total annual amount you want to save in each fund:

$____________________

÷12

= Amount to automate from each paycheck:

$____________________

FILL ME IN

If you're paid twice a month:

Total annual amount you want to save in each fund:

$________________________

÷24

= Amount to automate from each paycheck:

$________________________

If you're paid every other week:

Total annual amount you want to save in each fund:

$________________________

÷26

= Amount to automate from each paycheck:

$________________________

If you have inconsistent income:

If you're a freelancer, or otherwise have an irregular income, automating withdrawals to your sinking funds is a bit trickier. One option is to set up automatic transfers from your checking account monthly, bimonthly, etc., but if your paychecks don't arrive on a consistent schedule, you could be wading into dangerous overdrawing territory. Another option is to bank with a checking account that allows you to automatically save whenever money gets deposited into your account—Qapital (again, they're not paying me, you do you) has a "set and forget" rule that does this. Regardless of how you choose to do it, the important thing is that you make it as automated as you can, because part of feeling wealthy means thinking about your money as little as possible.

When committing to ridding your life of cheap habits, it's okay to go slow and not bite off more than you can chew. You are not going to untangle yourself from the lure of fast fashion, unlearn patterns of behavior, or have fully funded sinking funds overnight. Start with one area where you want to live more abundantly, such as putting $15 a week into a sinking fund specifically for hosting a monthly dinner party, or unfollowing accounts and unsubscribing from brands that make you feel tempted to overbuy fast-fashion items. Commit to the notion that all of these things take time—which means they are worth working toward.

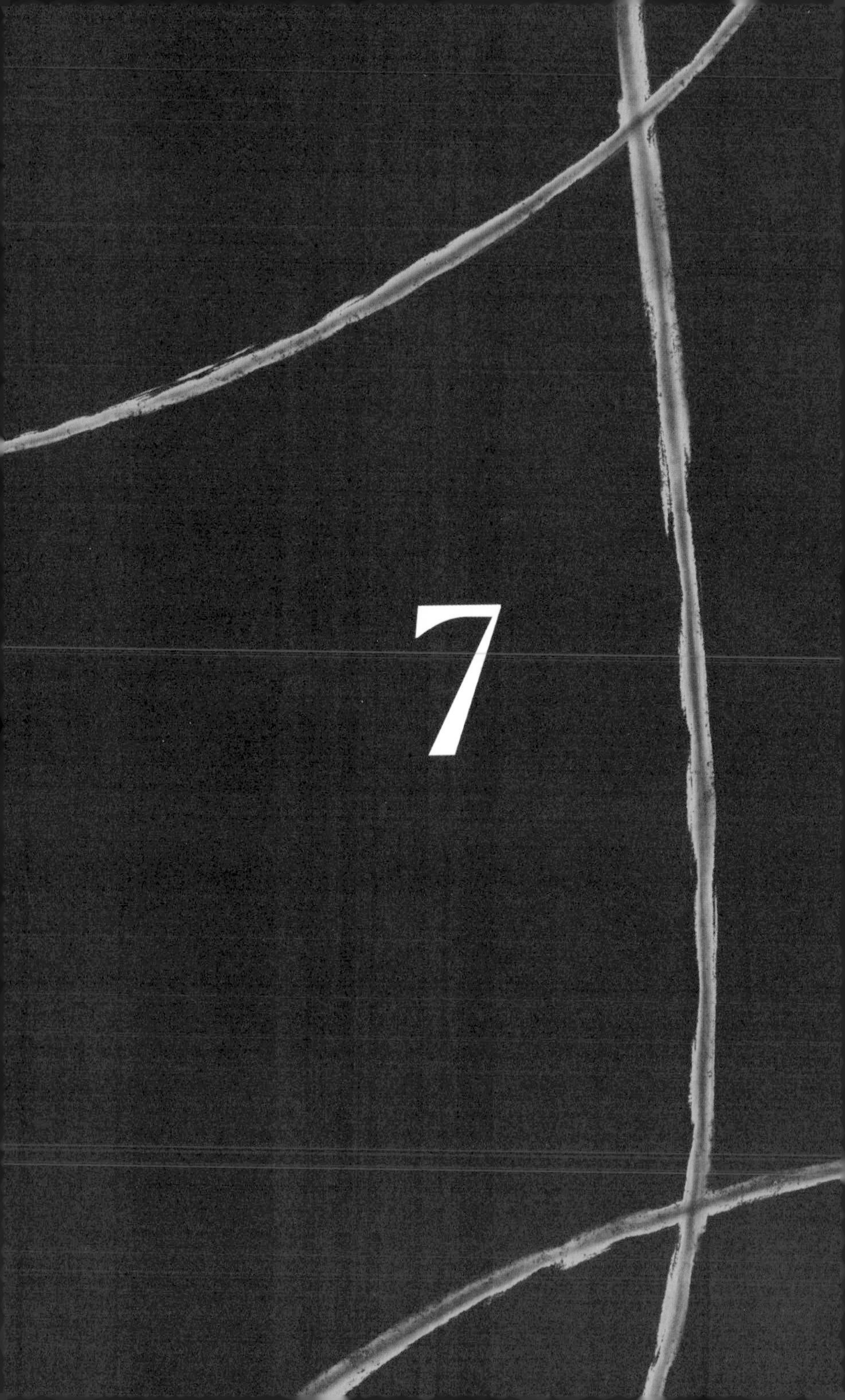

7

HOW TO MANIFEST WITHOUT THE GWYNETH PALTROW ENERGY

After internalizing a shame-free budgeting mindset and tweaking bigger-picture money strategies like your investments and debt payoff, the next natural step is to start actively working on building up your income. Like I discussed with the idea of defining your own personal happiness threshold, the goal here is not to earn as much as possible—it's to work toward an income that would help make your ideal life a reality. But for those of us who don't work in "elite" career fields where six-figure salaries, stock options, and absurdly high signing bonuses are commonplace, growing a higher income doesn't necessarily have a cut-and-dried path.

And when it comes to advice about growing your income, nothing grinds my gears more than hearing empty platitudes on earning more through the "law of attraction," sometimes referred to as money manifesting. It's not a new concept: The book *The Secret* came out in 2006 and popularized the idea that you can think something into belief by putting the thought of it out into the universe. There is some science to back the power of visualization, but the concept of manifesting has turned into a catchall explanation for how a specific type of person gained their financial success. How did your classmate who barely graduated land a high-paying consulting job right out of college? How did a socialite get a seven-figure book deal for her memoir? How did a Mormon mommy blogger gain millions of TikTok followers? By manifesting it into existence, of course!

Manifesting: Wellness Culture's Answer to Bootstrapping

Among wellness gurus, "manifestation" is touted as an almost spiritual practice; they posit that if you just visualize and vocalize your goals enough, they will come true. That may sound harmless until you consider that if manifestation is the answer, the opposite must also be true: that if you don't manifest hard enough, you're simply not worthy of success. In this way, wellness culture has become almost a replacement for organized religion in our modern-day lives. We've swapped living by the principles of a gospel with living by the principles of "wellness," an infuriatingly meaningless term that has somehow been assigned significant meaning. Under wellness culture, we've learned the importance of "clean eating," finding the most optimal exercise routine, meditating, and manifesting in order to achieve self-actualization. Yet just like Evangelical principles rooted in shame, wellness culture's idea of manifesting often glosses over the financial and systemic issues that affect each of us differently. And this, once again, makes some of us believe that success and financial status are outcomes tied to our own inherent abilities and worthiness—even though the people who are actually able to reap the benefits of manifestation likely had some substantial privilege in the first place.

Manifesting is the equivalent of what bootstrapping has been for the Dave Ramseys of the world. Using a bootstrapping-centric, shame-based approach to finances, those men argue they got where they are simply through hard work and perseverance, rather than acknowledging what they've obtained through privilege and luck. Similarly, manifesting has provided an opportunity for already-wealthy, conventionally attractive, typically white women to explain how they got where they are without once acknowledging the money, connections, and other privileges that gave them a leg (or three) up. The advice is different, but both perspectives ignore personal and systemic limitations, equating financial success with your inherent worth as a person. And they have the same ultimate end goal: to sell us bullshit.

And really, no one has exemplified the problems with selling wellness cures and manifestation advice more than beloved nepo baby Gwyneth Paltrow.

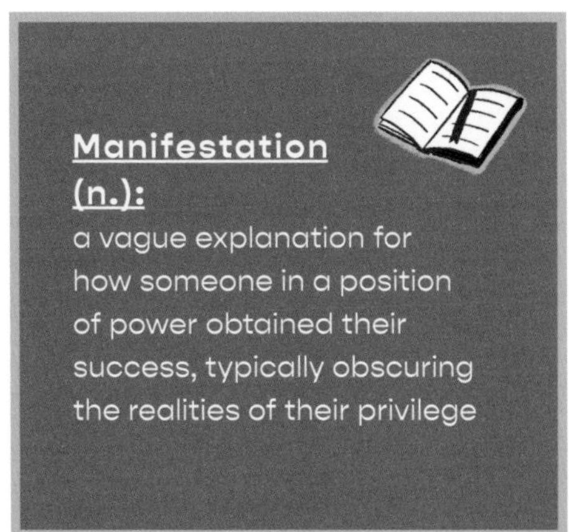
Manifestation (n.):
a vague explanation for how someone in a position of power obtained their success, typically obscuring the realities of their privilege

Why Is Gwyneth Paltrow Giving Me Money Advice?

A Hollywood actress turned lifestyle guru, Gwyneth

Visualization is a tool used in competitions by professional athletes, such as golfers Tiger Woods and Jack Nicklaus (I know, a sports reference—I'm as shocked as you are!). But it's not that they visualize themselves winning: They visualize exactly how each individual shot is going to play out. Muhammad Ali used the same practice in boxing, calling it "mental rehearsal." The focus is not visualizing the outcome of a goal, but rather visualizing the process of what it will take to achieve it.

Paltrow has long been a face of self-optimization in the name of wellness, from her cookbooks focusing on "clean" recipes to publicizing her transcendental meditation practice. And for a long time, part of Gwyneth's public persona has involved touting the virtues of manifesting the life you want into existence. On the web pages of her lifestyle brand, Goop, you'll find articles and podcast episodes with titles like "How to Be a Super Attractor and Manifest the Life You Want" and "10 Wellness Gurus on Tools for Manifesting Positive Outcomes." Some of the tips listed include lighting incense, using essential oils, undergoing ear acupuncture, and focusing on feeling good so you receive feel-good experiences in return. Instead of providing evidence-based research and citing sources, the wellness advice you can find on Goop is filled with oversimplified quick fixes, plus plenty of links to products they sell directly. And note that money is never mentioned: The end goal is always something like "manifesting the life you want," never acknowledging that an ideal life is inherently tied to building wealth. That would be gauche.

It's not just that Goop's success tactics and Gwyneth's wellness advice feel out of touch with reality. The company has been known to sell products and popularize practices under the guise of wellness that are often accused of being rooted in pseudoscience. Someone doing the Lord's work once cross-checked all the products Goop sold that were also for sale on the Infowars website. Infowars is a far-right, conspiratorial media company hosted by a man who is both the aesthetic and cultural opposite of Gwyn—yet both companies seem to attract audiences who are willing to buy into pseudoscience and hearsay.

Goop even landed itself in a lawsuit, settling for $145,000, after it started selling a now-infamous jade vagina egg (!) with the promise that it would help balance hormones and strengthen your pelvic floor. (It's still for sale, with a few key copy changes on the webpage to avoid making unsubstantiated claims about the health benefits of the egg.) As I'm writing this in the spring of 2023, Gwyneth is under fire for a handful of controversies, including a podcast interview with her doctor, a functional medicine expert and chiropractor who does not have an M.D. During the podcast, she mentions trying "rectal Ozone therapy," a practice that is not approved by the FDA and has not been proven to have any benefits. Through the entire interview, Gwyn is hooked up to an IV drip, at one point mentioning that her favorite "hard to find" IV is phosphatidylcholine—a chemical most of us can easily get in our diet by eating things like eggs and soybeans. She discusses how she eats bone broth for lunch most days and otherwise sticks to a paleo diet to support her "detox," which is a controversial diet regimen. Goop also currently sells its own detox starter kit, with a product description that claims to help customers start removing processed foods from their diet—with a weeklong elimination program that includes a protein powder, i.e., a processed food.

So why is Gwyneth still so successful? Why is Goop able to land Netflix docuseries and Audible Originals contracts and sell tickets to annual "wellness" weekend retreats for $4,500 a pop? It has not happened because Gwyneth speaks her truth to power, tells the universe what she wants, builds a healthy sense of self-worth, or however else she wants to describe manifesting. It is because she is a massive A-list celebrity descended from other celebrities (and is the literal goddaughter of Steven Spielberg) who's had a hugely successful brand for years on top of her megawatt acting career. Her success was foretold by her financial privilege and professional dominance well before she pivoted to selling vaginal eggs, so much so that even those controversies couldn't disrupt her ascension. She didn't manifest; she followed the clearly defined path laid before her by her privilege.

According to Ryan Houlihan, journalist, drag artist, and co-host of TFD's podcast *Too Good to Be True*, it's easy for people to buy into Gwyneth's and Goop's false health claims, bad financial advice, and cringey sales tactics because she is all the things society values: conventionally beautiful, rich, and white. "The more outrageously spoiled and privileged and completely removed from the filthy human experience she presents herself," they say, "the more delicious the escapist fantasy of being her becomes." And when her core audience is other people from substantial privilege, her out-of-touch persona doesn't actually cost her anything.

> **"Ultimately, the nepo baby discourse only gives Gwyneth more positive attention from the audience she's actually monetizing: people like her."**

Again, some of the woo-woo concepts of manifesting that you see on sites like Goop are not harmful in a vacuum. I wouldn't dare take your incense from you if it truly adds value to your life (though it should be noted that Goop seems to make a habit of co-opting and profiting off of Eastern spirituality practices, with the express purpose of padding the pockets of an already-rich white woman). But the idea that you can simply will something into reality by being positive, or worse, by buying such-and-such herbal remedy, isn't actually helpful, especially when the struggling person buying it doesn't have preexisting wealth or connections. So, if you look at people like Gwyneth and feel annoyed, or even angered, that their advice for manifesting the success you want sounds easier said than done, you are right to feel that way.

The term **"nepo baby"** has become shorthand for anyone who got a leg up because their parents were already successful in a certain industry. We typically associate nepo babies with the entertainment industry (Sofia Coppola, Jaden Smith, Zoë Kravitz, Miley Cyrus, etc.), but don't be fooled: They are everywhere among us. And according to Ryan Houlihan, resenting spoiled young people is nothing new—social media has just made it easier to talk about.

"The generation consuming the bulk of this content is also coming into a world of exponential wealth inequality and rampant worker exploitation," they say. "If your advantages in life only exist because you're exploiting other people (or someone is exploiting people on your behalf), you can't reasonably expect those same people to celebrate your success. People don't resent nepo babies for who they are; they resent the fact that many of the advantages given to the wealthy are artificial and rest entirely on racist, misogynistic, queerphobic, and classist institutions designed specifically to extract money from the poor and give it back to the rich."

This is the exact reason why, starting in 2022, we saw a social media reckoning of calling out nepo babies—in Hollywood and elsewhere—for what they are. No one wants to hear you talk about how hard you've worked or how much positive energy you've put into the universe to achieve your dreams when your privileges meant your dreams were a foregone conclusion. And you don't have to be Hollywood royalty for this to apply to you. Ivy League legacy admissions, inheritances from wealthy relatives, and even just a foot in the door at your dad's friend's corporate office are examples of privileges you don't have to do anything to earn; ignoring the impact of those privileges on your personal success is a total cop-out.

But I'm not going to spend the rest of this book dwelling on Gwyneth and other products of nepotism, because the problem extends well beyond her. I simply don't believe it's possible to attribute *any* success to skill, hard work, or positive-thinking tactics alone. There are rare exceptions, but most of us must acknowledge the circumstances that helped us learn a certain skill, gave us time to work hard, or allowed us to think positively in the first place. But when it comes to growing your income, instead of manifesting, the key is facilitating: leveraging what you already have to work with.

Manifestation vs. Facilitation

The idea of manifesting suggests an ease that can really only exist if you already have substantial privilege at your disposal, usually in the form of money. So if manifesting means simply radiating positivity and visualizing your desires into reality, then facilitation is a much more pragmatic and intentional way to put the ideas behind manifestation into practice. It involves the process of visualizing not just the outcome you want, but the process it's going to take to get there. Someone who is good at money facilitation is not inherently more talented or more deserving than anyone else. She has simply mastered putting herself out there until she gets what she wants—and that, in itself, is a skill. So how did she get there?

When we question why people who come from generational wealth have a grasp on money manifestation, the answer is usually quite simple.

They were born into the kind of entitlement and safety net that allows them to seize professional opportunities, like starting a lifestyle brand with no appropriate experience or credentials, without thinking twice about whether it's a good idea. In order to facilitate more income, having a lot of money to start with is a huge boon, but it's not a universal prerequisite. Income facilitation is about visualizing the *steps* that will help you reach your earning goal, and then actually following through with them.

Whenever you're setting out to reach a goal, it's always good to write out all the steps it will take you to achieve it, then categorize them by how much time and energy they'll take you. For instance, the lowest-energy, lowest-lift steps are the ones you'll often want to tackle first. We like to think of these as the low-hanging fruit of the goal-planning process—things you can put on your to-do list within the next week or so. When it comes to facilitating more income, some examples could be:

- reconnecting with a former colleague you have mutual respect with to see if they know of potential opportunities
- buying a domain name for your side project or freelance business
- cleaning up your résumé or LinkedIn page
- scheduling a call with a trusted friend from your field to talk through side income stream ideas
- setting up a social media profile and email marketing account for your freelance work
- researching your job's market rate
- starting a list of "work wins" to take with you to your next performance review (which I'll be diving into more deeply in the next chapter!)

In debt payoff, the "snowball" method has gained substantial popularity because it has you tackle your smallest debts first before aiming to pay off your biggest ones. In the same vein, starting with low-hanging fruit, or easy wins, is a good tactic for reaching any goal; when you see small successes happen quickly, it motivates you to keep going.

The next category of income facilitation steps is things that take slightly more time and energy. These are things you can add to your schedule over the next month, such as:

- growing your list of potential freelance contacts to cold email and getting started on your outreach
- maintaining a running list of job opportunities from your company's competitors (especially if you're an hourly employee)
- publishing a few TikToks on your area of expertise
- prepping for and setting up a meeting with your manager to discuss your salary goals for the year
- setting up a session with a salary negotiation coach
- sending out your first marketing email and creating a plan for building up your email list
- building out a basic website on Squarespace

Finally, there are the biggest-lift items that take a lot of energy or forethought (or both), which you can schedule over the next few months. These might look like:

- building out your social media marketing calendar
- signing up for a professional certificate class or training program
- asking to be added to a new project at work
- offering (and carrying out) your services to a friend pro bono to gain more experience
- regularly networking with people in your industry
- fleshing out your website and implementing your email building strategy
- regularly cold emailing potential clients and asking for testimonials from existing ones

FILL ME IN

Visualizing Your Income Facilitation Plan

Manifesting money means visualizing what you want and voicing it, and with defining your happiness threshold, you've already done that. When you facilitate money, you have to think intentionally about *how* you're going to get what you want. Below are some steps to create an income facilitation plan to help you envision what's going to get you closer to that happiness threshold.

Current State of the Income:

Your net annual income (including bonuses/commissions):	
Amount per month:	
Your monthly happiness threshold (amount you want to earn more per year, divided by 12):	

Now, there are two main methods to increase your income: increasing your main salary or adding or expanding a secondary income stream. Later on in this book, I'll cover tackling some internalized insecurities to help you approach any negotiation with confidence. But of course, before you reach the negotiation phase, you must decide *what* you're negotiating. Below are two exercises to help you determine your best course of action.

FILL ME IN

Growing a main income stream:

When was the last time you got a raise? Is it time to negotiate one?	
What are your industry norms for pay increases?	
Should you be looking at other employers instead of just negotiating within your current company? What are your other employment options?	
What's your goal for increasing your main income source in the next six months?	

Adding or expanding an income stream:

Are you currently accruing any additional income? If so, how much, and is it passive or active?	
Are there any clear opportunities to increase this existing income that you're not currently taking advantage of? (This may be a good opportunity to ask a friend or peer in the same space!)	

FILL ME IN

What are some ways you could start diversifying your income streams in the next six months? What kind of time commitments or up-front investments would they require? This is a space for brain dumping, not decision-making, so list anything you can think of here.	
Which of those income sources feels most realistic to facilitate in the next six months? (For this, consider income streams that utilize your existing expertise or skill set.)	
What's your goal for increasing your side income in the next six months, either from expanding an existing income stream or from adding a new one?	

Next, use the visualization activity below to help you map out these short-, medium-, and long-term steps to intentionally grow your income.

Growing a main income stream:

Are there any skills or certifications you could add to increase your value at your current place of work, or to other employers?	
Low-hanging fruit: What can you do in the next week to get closer to your six-month goal?	
Needs a bit more planning: What can you do in the next month to get closer to your six-month goal?	
Involves significant time and energy: What can you do in the next three months to get closer to your six-month goal?	

FILL ME IN

Adding or expanding an income stream:

If you're adding or expanding an income stream based on your current expertise and skills, what is currently standing in your way? (Marketing, web presence, creating necessary connections, etc.)	
Low-hanging fruit: What can you do in the next week to get closer to your six-month goal?	
Needs a bit more planning: What can you do in the next month to get closer to your six-month goal?	
Involves significant time and energy: What can you do in the next three months to get closer to your six-month goal?	

Of course, most of us weren't born in Gwyneth Paltrow's shoes. But I would argue that shoes like hers aren't all that aspirational in the first place—as we discovered earlier, endless wealth isn't a guaranteed path to happiness or self-actualization. However, putting visualization and manifestation techniques into practice shouldn't be reserved for the already rich. There's nothing inherently more special about the Gwyneths of the world; they simply have built-in platforms and lots of privilege that they've learned how to leverage. You may not have access to the same size platform or resources, but that doesn't mean you can't employ the resources and connections you *do* have at your disposal.

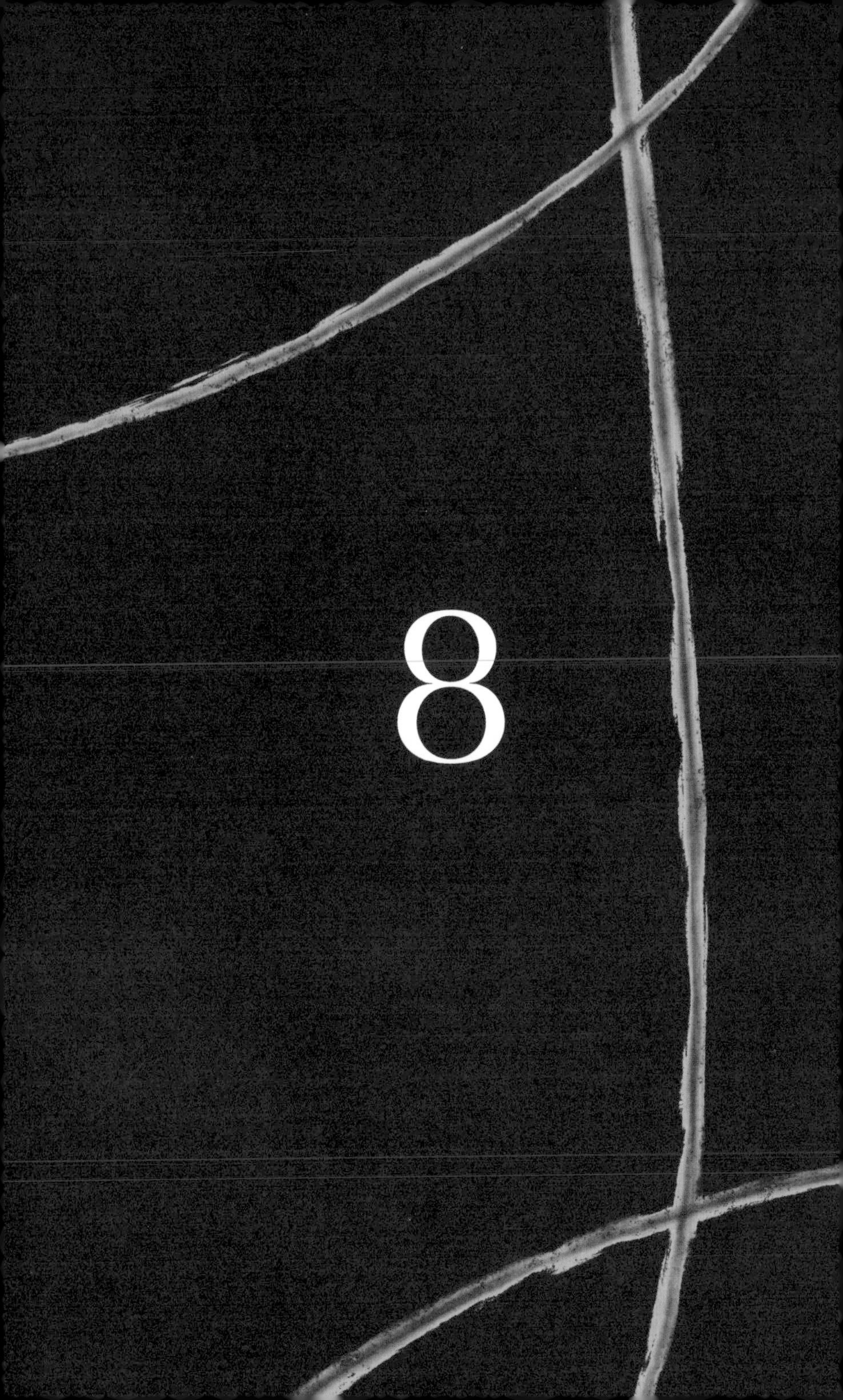

8

IMPOSTER SYNDROME, UNEARNED CONFIDENCE, AND NEGOTIATING UP

Making a plan to increase your income isn't necessarily easy or straightforward, but it's something most of us know how to do—at least in theory. For a lot of us, though, feeling confident about that plan is a whole different story. But without confidence, following through and negotiating for what you want is all but impossible. And no matter what plan you set in motion, or how hard you try, or how much your work speaks for itself, we all have to master the balancing act of negotiating in order to get anywhere close to what we deserve to be paid. Unfortunately, we get in our own way much of the time, thanks to imposter syndrome.

Who Experiences Imposter Syndrome?

Imposter syndrome has been talked about since at least 1978, when psychologists Pauline Rose Clance and Suzanne Imes released the first known study on the concept, titled "The Imposter Phenomenon in High Achieving Women: Dynamics and Therapeutic Intervention." Here's an excerpt from the study's abstract:

> **"Certain early family dynamics and later introjection of societal sex-role stereotyping appear to contribute significantly to the development of the imposter phenomenon. Despite outstanding academic and professional accomplishments, women who experience the imposter phenomenon persist in believing that they are really not bright and have fooled anyone who thinks otherwise. Numerous achievements, which one might expect to provide ample objective evidence of superior intellectual functioning, do not appear to affect the imposter belief."**

If educated, professionally successful, and (considering this original study was conducted in the seventies) presumably white women already experience such a high level of imposter syndrome, logic would follow that more marginalized people would experience imposter syndrome even more acutely. The experience of imposter syndrome is certainly not limited to one type of person, but it seems to show up in women more than men; a study conducted by global consulting firm KPMG found that 75% of female executives have experienced imposter syndrome at some point in their careers. Market research technology firm InnovateMR found that age is a significant factor as well, affecting 53% of women between the ages of twenty-five and thirty-four. Plus, much of the reason behind the development of imposter syndrome can be attributed to how you're treated in the workplace; if you're constantly undermined and having your credentials questioned, it is only natural to question your own sense of self-worth. For that reason, women of color, and specifically Black women, unfortunately have often experienced high levels of imposter syndrome.

I spoke with one of TFD's go-to career experts, professional recruiter and career coach Jazmine Reed, to get to the bottom of why that is. For women of color, first-generation immigrants, and other marginalized groups, "there's this idea that you should just be 'happy to be here,' so sit down and eat your piece of cake," she said. And when it comes to negotiating, this can work in the company's favor—not yours. Imposter syndrome triggers what Jazmine calls "good-girl conditioning," or the self-doubt that comes with being

How we're treated can influence our self-worth and cause us to feel imposter syndrome. A report from LeanIn.org titled "The State of Black Women in Corporate America" found that 41% of Black women have had their judgment questioned in their area of expertise, followed closely by 39% of white women, but significantly exceeding just 29% of all men. And 40% of Black women have had to provide evidence of their competence in the workplace, compared with 28% of white women and 14% of all men.

made to feel like you're lucky to have been given an opportunity in the first place.

Recently, Jazmine worked with a client who'd been at her company for twenty-five years and was being laid off after an acquisition. Her company originally wanted to give her just twelve weeks of severance, but Jazmine worked with her to negotiate sixteen. To Jazmine, it seemed obvious that her client deserved a better package. "She'd been there over twenty-five years, she was one of the first hires, she started off as receptionist and ended as an HR business partner, she's helped the company with $10 million deals," Jazmine said. "But still, she said, 'Yeah, but I don't have a college degree, and they took a chance on me, and who am I to ask for anything?'" The biggest hurdle the client had to overcome? Talking up her own value.

> **"She was struggling with feeling like it was braggadocious to go back and say, 'Look at all the things I've done.' And I think that again goes back to good-girl conditioning: Be happy you're here, don't ever take up more space than you're told."**

I mentioned that I've experienced imposter syndrome before, and it's true: I was not born with a natural sense of confidence in any situation. Despite being raised by a mom who always preached being your own best advocate, it took me years to internalize it. But I eventually learned to silence, or at least turn down the volume on, the little voice in my head telling me I'm not talented or smart enough to get where I've gotten. The truth isn't simply that I am; it's that when we experience imposter syndrome, we're often comparing ourselves to people who have succeeded despite being mediocre at what they do. And yet, because they have some specific type of institutional recognition or years of experience that exceed our own, we assume they are people to be intimidated by—even when the opposite is often true.

Of course, I don't know what it's like to navigate the workplace as a woman of color, a queer person, or an immigrant or child of immigrants, so I can only speak to my situation and observations as a straight, cisgender, white, U.S.-born woman. What I do have is plenty of experience navigating an industry of peers whose lives are at least partially funded by their parents well into adulthood (gotta love that New York City media scene, baby!). And I've found myself in more than one situation as the only person without a degree from an Ivy League college or prestigious journalism school. It has taught me that if you're worried about how much you deserve to take up space in your company or industry, you're likely *more* deserving than the "successful" people you're surrounded by, simply because you care enough to think about how you're performing in the first place.

Owning Your Confidence and the Myth of Meritocracy

The idea that many, if not most, successful people are mediocre may sound like hating from outside the club, but I find it to be a comforting thought when it comes to advocating for yourself and negotiating what you're worth. At TFD, we've had a lot of mantras over the years, but one we've turned to time and again is that no one is going to care about *your* money more than you do.

In order to put yourself out there and facilitate what you deserve, there's one thing everyone needs: a healthy dose of nihilism. I don't mean you need to become that guy at the college basement party going off about Nietzsche. I'm just asking you to entertain the possibility that nothing *really* matters. Not as an excuse to burn bridges or treat people like crap or commit a white-collar crime, but as an excuse to stop caring about what might happen *if*. It's like that meme of the two guys on a bus. You could be looking out the window at the steep, rocky mountainside, thinking that if nothing matters, there's no point

in trying to achieve anything. Or, you could choose to look out at the beautiful, sunlit mountain range, thinking that if nothing matters, there's no reason *not to try*.

Now, don't conflate this with the manifestation guru advice to simply let go of negative self-talk, as if it's possible to ignore the cultural, social, or financial disadvantages you've experienced. Not everything is going to be achievable, and it's not helpful to hold yourself to that standard. Most "successful" people got to where they are by simply being born on third base, and the sooner you internalize that, the sooner you can stop feeling like they're somehow more deserving than you are.

But there is plenty that is *not* out of reach, even if it feels like it. It is maddening to think of all those glorified frat bros taking up desk space in high-end finance and law firms simply because their dad's golf buddy worked there, but it should also be freeing.

The idea that we have "equal opportunity" is bullshit. More and more jobs require college degrees, despite their being out of reach for most people. According to the advocacy group Opportunity@Work, 75% of new job listings require a bachelor's degree, even though only 40% of potential applicants have one. And that disparity is just getting worse, as college enrollment dropped to a fifty-year low during the pandemic.

And while access to opportunities like a college degree are social class issues, we can't ignore the intersection of social class and race, and who ends up getting more of those opportunities. A 2021 Insight Center report found that white people have largely benefited from U.S. government programs in the past that Black people and other non-white ethnic groups have not: "The Homestead Act of 1862 helped white Americans settle the West—not through trailblazing and individualist spirit, but through the U.S. government distributing 270 million acres of (Native American) land to 1.5 million white families. Studies have found that at least 45 million white Americans today still benefit from that act."

Going back to Gwyneth, if she can keep putting out cookbooks with sketchy diet suggestions despite giving off extreme cannot-cook energy and having no nutrition credentials, goodness gracious, you are allowed to ask for a pay increase, or look for a different hourly job with a better rate, or turn down a freelance client who's unwilling to meet your minimum rate. If so many people got where they are because of where they were born, there's nothing that says they deserve it more than you do. They've never felt like there wasn't enough money to go around, so you shouldn't either.

And for what it's worth, you've likely already proven yourself a valuable addition to whatever team you're on. If you ever experience a lack of confidence, it is *highly probable* that it has nothing to do with how capable you are (and if you've ever had to fix a PowerPoint for your boss who couldn't figure out how to copy and paste . . . deep down, you already know I'm right). I truly believe anyone who picks up a book on living more abundantly and intentionally is already an introspective, considerate, conscientious person, i.e., exactly the kind of person others want to hire and work with.

Let's revisit Jazmine's conversation with her client who needed to negotiate a severance package. When Jazmine asked what her client's work best friend would say about her, her client lit up: Her professional strengths just started flowing out of her. But while trying to see yourself through the eyes of others is often helpful in these situations, hopefully you can get to a place where it's not necessary. "With imposter syndrome, and with women specifically, playing the long game and getting ahead of the problem is really the key," Jazmine said. "It's keeping that career journal, pulling the reports so that you can speak to your accomplishments during those performance reviews."

Jazmine also says that women tend to be good at cultivating and maintaining relationships, based on both how we've been socialized and how society views vulnerability in every kind of relationship as a "feminine" characteristic. Whether good or bad, she suggests using that to your advantage. "Start cultivating those strong relationships and key

FILL ME IN

Quick Reflection

When was a time you had to explain a process, tech-related or otherwise, to someone above you at work? Write any you can think of below:

partnerships with people at work" so that when it comes time to negotiate for yourself, it "doesn't feel so transactional and awkward."

And perhaps most importantly when it comes to negotiating, remember that a company is acting in its own best interest, and so should you. I like to think of this as "negotiating up." You're not asking for money from a friend or loved one or haggling for a lower rate from an already underpaid freelancer. You're asking for money from a business that can, more likely than not, afford to pay you more. And don't just think in terms of your current self—you're playing the long game. As Jazmine puts it:

> **"At the end of the day, a company is never going to overpay you. If it's a for-profit business, you're never gonna get more than you really deserve, in 99% of situations, anyway. Remind yourself that no matter what you have earned, you ultimately are giving up a third of your life to this company. Sometimes what helps me is to think of all the money you're going to leave on the table and how it compounds over time. Maybe you think, 'This is awkward. I'm not even gonna ask—it's two more grand, what's it really worth?' But what is two grand worth over the course of the rest of your career? How much money could you be leaving on the table?"**

One effective way to internalize confidence is to think about things that come easily to you. They might be obvious parts of your job, or supplemental parts—but ask yourself, *Which tasks feel second nature to me, especially if my colleagues seem to struggle with them?* Whatever your answers are, remind yourself that these aren't tasks you should take for granted; they are skills, and oftentimes, they make you an absolute asset.

For instance, I'm good at production management, from always knowing a project's status, to scheduling filming sessions and sending out video footage ahead of time, to giving final notes. Those are hardly the extent of my work responsibilities, but they are the things I always seem to manage without having to think about them. And a lot of the time, they don't even make it onto my to-do list, because I've already taken care of them. Once you identify your own second-nature skills, you'll have a much easier time voicing your workplace value. I promise. This isn't to say you can't be good at something you find difficult—you absolutely can. But we tend to overvalue tasks we find stressful and undervalue tasks we find easy.

What a Raise Can Really Be Worth

Say your company wants to pay you $50,000, but you asked for $52,000. It may not seem like a huge difference, but you owe it to yourself to discover what $2,000 will be worth over the course of your career.

Starting at $50,000, and assuming you're getting a 3% raise every year on average, you'll be at a salary of $121,363.12 in thirty years. If you push for that extra $2,000 at the outset and assume the same level of raises, you'll be at $126,217.65 in thirty years. Again, not a *huge* increase for that one year, at a less-than-$5,000 difference in annual salary.

But when you have an extra two, three, or even $5,000 coming in every year, that can add up. In this scenario, the differences in salary each year would add up to over **$98,000** over the course of a thirty-year career—and that's assuming you likely never started a new job, got a promotion, or otherwise made a move that would get you an even larger raise.

FILL ME IN

Maintaining a Self-Advocacy Journal

Confidence isn't simply a tap you can turn on—it's a practice. You have to build it up in the first place, and then you must keep working at it so you don't lose it. As Jazmine mentioned, keeping a "career journal" is key for having something to turn to when you need to advocate for yourself, especially when asking for more money. Start an ongoing list of work wins in a Google doc or your notes app, and refer to it regularly. If you're at a loss when trying to think of anything worthwhile, use the following questions to help guide you. For each question, write down as many applicable examples as you can think of.

What parts of your job do you find so easy you don't have to think about them?

What positive feedback have you received from your manager, a client/customer, or a coworker?

What is a key company or department metric that has improved since you started in your role?

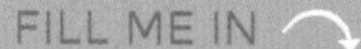

FILL ME IN

What is a workflow practice, policy, or system you implemented or improved? What impact has it had on your company/clients?

Have you brought in any new clients or facilitated any other important connections?

What is a part of your job that makes other people's jobs easier?

Freelancing and Putting a Price on Your Time

When you're negotiating for a raise at a current job or negotiating as part of the hiring process, there's already a lot of information at your disposal. You can research your job's market rate on a site like Glassdoor or PayScale and ask your friends what their salaries are and how they negotiated them. (And this goes without saying, but you should freely offer that information to friends when asked, because talking about money is a two-way street!) In some places, like the state of California and New York City, businesses are required by law to post salary ranges on their job listings.

You might be thinking, *Can I get fired for sharing my salary?* While you can't fully control how an employer might react if you share what they consider "confidential" information, *most* employers must abide by the National Labor Relations Act, which asserts that policies specifically prohibiting discussing wages are unlawful. You can find out if you are protected under this act at nlrb.gov.

But putting a price on your time isn't so clear-cut when it comes to setting freelance rates. For instance, say you decide to do some consulting on the side, putting your UX design expertise to work outside your nine-to-five job. You may calculate an hourly rate by dividing your annual salary by 52 (the number of weeks in a year) and 40 (or however many hours you work in a week). That number might give you what your hourly rate is at your primary job, but when it comes to setting freelance rates, it might not quite cut it. For one thing, you may be underpaid at your current job, or a simple hourly rate based on your own or a market salary isn't going to include the extra work and costs that come with being a freelancer.

According to Jazmine Reed, the first (and often most overlooked) step is to include the administrative tasks and strategy-building time that allow you to work on a freelance project. That includes the hours spent marketing yourself and finding clients, following up on emails, outsourcing your bookkeeping and taxes, building up a website, and much more. "That's why I had to raise my rates," she told me. "I realized that by the time I was done sending the emails, doing the invoices, doing research sometimes for certain projects, I'd maybe cut my rate in half."

As a thoughtful and generous person, however, you might find yourself feeling guilty asserting what your rates are. That's totally understandable, and there might be instances where it makes sense to offer someone a lower rate for your service. But you don't want to make a habit of underselling yourself. Often, the entire point of freelancing is to have more freedom, so what's the purpose of working for yourself if you end up having to work even *longer* hours than at a full-time job simply because you set your own rates too low? But if you're struggling with feeling guilty that you can't give more of yourself, Jazmine suggests finding some middle ground and coming up with something you can offer to people who can't afford you. For her, this looks like free career resources she shares on her website and social media.

FILL ME IN

Setting the Correct Freelance Rate

Reflect on the questions below to help demystify the process of setting the right freelance rate.

1. What is your current hourly rate as a freelancer? (Even if you set project-based rates for clients, refer to what you consider your hourly rate in your own mind.) Leave blank and skip to question 3 if you are just starting out on a freelance journey.	
2. How many hours a week do you spend on administrative tasks (cold outreach, email, invoicing, project management, etc.) vs. working on projects directly?	
3. What is the annual "salary" you want to make, based on the market salary for someone with your job title in a full-time employee position?	
4. What are the total yearly costs you incur as a freelancer that you wouldn't as an employee (healthcare, bookkeeping and	

FILL ME IN

taxes, LLC and legal fees, unpaid vacation time, etc.)? Add these costs on top of your ideal annual salary.	
5. How many hours a week do you want to work on average, excluding administrative time? How much time off do you want to take during the year? Add up the total hours you want to work directly on projects in a year.	
6. Take your new ideal salary (ideal salary + extra freelance costs) and divide it by the total hours you want to work annually (total hours worked minus admin time minus vacation time). This is your new hourly rate!	

If you don't have a good grasp on how long you spend on various tasks, scan this code to get access to TFD's time audit spreadsheet to track your work hours for the next few weeks:

Hourly Jobs and Hitting the Wage Wall

A lot of negotiation advice applies mainly to people who have salaried jobs, leaving hourly, tipped, and gig workers out of the equation. Unfortunately, earning more in these roles is often much further out of your control than in salaried or even freelance jobs. The already-low federal minimum wage is usually even less for tipped workers based on their state. While some states are working toward raising their minimum wages, there's still often little you can do about what a company is willing to pay.

As an hourly worker, what you *can* do is learn to negotiate opportunities and leverage your skills and expertise. Currently, Jazmine is working in high-volume recruiting for an e-commerce business filling positions in their fulfillment centers. While other companies she's worked with in the past have had wiggle room in the wages offered based on years of experience and other factors, her current company doesn't—the rate is the rate, full stop. So what do you do if you're in such a job and are unable to negotiate a higher rate simply because of company policy? Here's what Jazmine says:

> **"It really comes down to negotiating opportunities. I know that's not the most satisfying answer, because people think, *Great, so you want me to take on more work for free in the short term, with the hope that it is prosperous long term.* But leverage the different opportunities you have. Make sure that you do find those really important relationships, because those are ultimately going to be your advocates and your sponsors."**

This is not to say that you should just be happy with being paid less than you deserve—it's simply about taking advantage of every opportunity at your disposal. "No matter if it's hourly or you're making six figures, wring dry the experience you can," Jazmine said. "Maybe it is knowing, *Hey, this is something I'm going to do for one year, and I'm going to garner X, Y, and Z skill sets out of it, and I'm going to make sure I get this person as a reference.* And then I would allow that to propel you into something in the future."

For tipped service workers, the hourly rate is often below the minimum wage; only seven states plus Guam require employers to pay tipped workers the state minimum wage *before* tips, while most others allow employers to subtract a "tip credit."

I learned the importance of being open to more hourly opportunities in college, when I worked an hourly job as a receptionist at my school. I would often hear of extra hours for certain events, like alumni receptions and school-sponsored conferences. I would *always* take them, because they would typically pay time and a half, and because they allowed me to showcase different skills that I didn't have the opportunity to use in my day-to-day job. That is the unfortunate reality for many hourly and gig workers, though: Earning more often means working more hours. But as Jazmine said, leveraging and negotiating opportunities might mean working more in the short term, but it could pay off in the long term, such as with a promotion to a management position, maybe even a salaried one.

The same sort of advice can apply to gig workers. Say you regularly take on projects from TaskRabbit. Do you have any return clients you could ask for testimonials or references? You never know what those connections could turn into, so try to foster relationships with customers as much as you can—at least, with customers who pass the vibe check. (At TFD, we have personal relationships with many types of contractors, from virtual assistants to video editors, and we always prefer working with people we already know we can rely on when starting a new project! Connections pay dividends.)

Plus, you may be able to leverage other opportunities by looking at the non-salary benefits your company has on offer. Companies like Chipotle, Discover, and Taco Bell are just a few that cover the full cost of tuition for certain degrees for qualifying employees. But also, don't be afraid to walk away. That means if there's a competitor offering better pay than your current hourly position, don't feel guilty jumping at that opportunity. At Jazmine's own company, "all the warehouses are literally on the same street. Something like thirteen people went next door to the next warehouse, because they were paying more. And they should have. The company is only going to look out for themselves. So just like they're their own best advocate, you have to be your own best advocate." Remember, that goes for programs like tuition reimbursement; it's certainly a perk for employees, but by enrolling, the company ensures you work for them the entire time you're in your program, with the aim of lowering costly turnover rates. Don't lose sight of the fact that you are valuable to your company, regardless of what your pay is. You don't owe them more than you signed up for, even if you take advantage of the benefits they offer.

FILL ME IN

Opportunity Negotiation Checklist

If you're an hourly employee, leveraging different opportunities may pay off in the long run. Use this checklist to see whether you're making the most of what you currently have available to you:

- [ ] Take the initiative to set up a quarterly touch-base with your manager to get feedback on your job performance.
- [ ] Before your yearly performance review, ask what you need to do in order to solidify a raise. Keep a running log of the tasks and responsibilities you've taken on (refer to the earlier "self-advocacy journal" exercise for help on what to track).
- [ ] See if there are any additional opportunities, hours, projects, etc., that you could sign on for.
- [ ] Ask if there is a management track or training opportunity, and if you're interested, ask what you can do to make yourself a standout candidate—then follow through.
- [ ] See if there are better-paying or otherwise more advantageous opportunities at other companies in your industry.

9

THE WOMAN WHO "HAS IT ALL," OUR GREATEST ENEMY

In the sixth circle of TikTok hell, you will find thousands of videos with eerily similar jokes. One will have text reading "My husband when he does one household chore" superimposed over a man taking out a bag of trash while adjusting his sunglasses and waving like a celebrity on a red carpet. The next will show a man taking a luxurious bath and napping the day away due to his "man cold" as his wife keeps the kids entertained while simultaneously making dinner and doing the laundry. Yet another will show a man frantically trying to figure out how he's going to get a full night's sleep in a hospital chair, filmed from the perspective of his wife who is several hours into labor.

Women spend over 16 hours a week on domestic labor—5.5 *more* hours than men. The one task men spend more time on than women? Lawn and garden care.

At TFD, we've termed this "adult toddler husband content," but it's hardly a new dynamic. For decades, we have witnessed the sitcom trope of the useless husband and the (usually much more conventionally attractive) nagging wife, spanning shows from *Happy Days* in the 1970s to the more recent *Modern Family*. Aren't we supposed to laugh because it's true? Married moms have long complained, jokingly or otherwise, that managing their husbands feels like taking care of an additional child. Despite the fact that American women have largely entered the workplace, representing over 46% of the labor force in the U.S. every year since 1995, they are still disproportionately taking on the majority of domestic labor—even when they work full-time. According to the 2021 American Time Use Survey from the U.S. Bureau of Labor Statistics, women spend 2.33 hours per day on household activities (housework, food preparation and cleanup, household management, and lawn and garden care) compared to 1.54 hours a day for men.

You would think that more women in the workforce would mean men would shoulder the burden of domestic labor at home, but no—women are just expected to take on more in every aspect. And in my humble opinion, this dynamic originates to one thing: chasing the idea of "having it all." Women are told to pursue their career goals the way men do but while *also* being expected to take care of all household management and childcare. Aspiring to have it all means women must take on the role of ringleader in every aspect of their lives, further unequally tipping the scale—and the trope of the nagging housewife and hapless husband is a natural consequence of women having to take on so much. Frankly, "having it all" has managed to convince us that oppression is somehow aspirational.

Important note: Most of this chapter will focus on women in heterosexual relationships, because to put it plainly, straight, cisgender men have not been socialized to concern themselves with household chores and management (speaking generally, of course). But I should note that while child-free same-sex couples seem to split domestic duties in more egalitarian ratios than heterosexual couples, there is still a clear divide that emerges when the couple has a child: The lower earner takes on the brunt of childcare duties.

According to a 2018 article from *The New York Times*, "When gay and lesbian couples have children, they often begin to divide things as heterosexual couples do. . . . Though the couples are still more equitable, one partner often has higher earnings, and one a greater share of household chores and child care. It shows these roles are not just about gender: Work and much of society are still built for single-earner families."

Dismantling the Independent-Career-Girlie-to-I-Married-an-Adult-Toddler Pipeline

Instead of asking ourselves why women taking on more responsibility in the workplace hasn't coincided with men taking on more domestic labor (because what's in it for them?), we must focus on what we can do to untangle ourselves from these conditions. And in order to do that, we must interrogate the ways we may be sabotaging our own domestic lives in the name of having it all.

The idea of having it all references the concept that women can have everything they want, from a thriving career to a fulfilling home life, from a happy marriage to a busy social life. But the term itself is quite vague. If you can *have* it all, it means someone has to actually *do* it all. And when we look at women's increased share of the labor force contrasted with their shouldering of the majority of household tasks, "doing it all" seems to fall on women alone.

Worse still, the origins of the term "having it all" speak only to one specific type of woman. The term was popularized by Helen Gurley Brown's (now quaint and at least slightly problematic) book *Having It All: Love, Success, Sex, Money . . . Even If You're Starting With Nothing*, first published in 1982. And as a popular author and the longtime editor of *Cosmopolitan*, Gurley Brown typifies the whitewashed version of the women's lib movement popularized in media: white, upper-middle to upper class, educated, and professional. Here's an excerpt from Jennifer Szalai's 2015 *New York Times Magazine* article dissecting the origins of the phrase "having it all":

> **"Ruth Rosen, a scholar who has written extensively about the history of feminism, [said] that you can't find much archival evidence of the phrase before the tail end of the 1970s—and even then, it wasn't so much a feminist mantra as a marketing pitch directed toward the well-heeled 'liberated' consumer. . . . To say that women**

expect to 'have it all' is to trivialize issues like parental leave, equal pay and safe, affordable child care; it makes women sound like entitled, narcissistic battle-axes while also casting them as fools."

To Gurley Brown's credit, the article mentions that she also didn't like the term for the name of the book but had to give in to publisher pressures. Nonetheless, "having it all" remains associated with women like her who, born into it or not, have obtained substantial class privilege. A wealthy, upwardly mobile, professional-class woman who doesn't have to shoulder the burden of childcare alone is likely going to have more time to worry about whether she's having it all compared to a working-class mom struggling to provide for her family.

But even for those successful, privileged career women, having it all (or, at least, the version of having it all that includes a husband who takes on his fair share of household tasks) has still proven to be a pipe dream. Researchers have found that when women are the breadwinners, they feel they have to overcompensate for taking over that male-coded role—and so they do more domestic labor to make up for it. This once again proves one of the central theses of this book: Having more money can certainly make your life easier, but it's not going to fix your life for you.

Rethinking What "Having It All" Means

Just like buying more fast-fashion clothing for less money doesn't mean living abundantly, the idea that you can have it all—that you can give 100% of yourself to every facet of your life—doesn't make room for more. It simply stretches you too thin; you only have 100% to give in the first place. Trying to be the quintessential PTA president soccer mom *and* the kickass entrepreneur *and* the Pilates devotee *and* the consummate dinner party host is a recipe for burnout and resenting your life. Add on top of that the probability of having a husband who won't take on domestic responsibilities without explicitly being asked, and you're going to end up doing everything for everyone.

When we think of having it all as being fully present in every facet of our lives, it's harmful to suggest that women can have it all in the first place, let alone that they should want to. "'To have' reflects consumption," says Tiffany Dufu, author of *Drop the Ball: Achieving More by Doing Less* and founder of women's peer coaching organization The Cru. "It's saying *I'm supposed to have it all, I'm supposed to possess it all,* when really life is about living, it's about the present." But that doesn't mean she thinks women, or anyone, can't thrive in all areas of life that matter to them.

"I actually believe that it's possible to be a really incredible mom or parent, that it's possible to be a really thoughtful, intentional partner, in my case wife, and to have a career that you love that's rooted in your passion and your purpose, and to be a good daughter and a good mentor, and to contribute to your church, or your synagogue—to actually be all of these things simultaneously, and to thrive," Tiffany says. "The challenge is, what does it mean to be any of those things? We're all born into our lives playing certain roles. If you were assigned 'girl' [at birth], your first role was probably daughter. If you had siblings, you became a sister. You went to the playground, you became a friend, a student, a worker, maybe a manager. At some point you might become a wife." In her work, she's also noted that it hasn't mattered what cultural background someone has: We all have very similar job descriptions for what it means to be a mom, a wife, a sister, etc.

And while everyone feels pressure when playing their various roles, mothers feel pressure to be "good" particularly acutely. In 2017, *Time* conducted a survey of 913 new moms, finding that 70% of them felt pressure to mother a certain way—i.e., they had a clearly defined idea of what a good mom was supposed to look like, influenced by their culture, family, society, and other external factors. Here's one example that Tiffany gave me about how people get stuck on an idea of perfect motherhood and how that can be harmful to our self-perception:

> **"In the job description for a good mom, you're gonna see something online that says you are required to be present when your child takes their first steps. I can't tell you the number of women I've spoken to who are really stressed because they have a work event that's going to take them out of the city, and the train leaves the station or the plane takes off, and their child, who is about a year old, is going to start walking. They will have missed this event. That doesn't mean they are a bad mom and not a good mom."**

It doesn't help that, as I previously mentioned, married mothers are likely quite alone in managing households and taking on parenting responsibilities. In fact, single and divorced mothers often have *more* free time than married mothers, and mothers with husbands often spend more time on housework. That's the issue with the adult toddler husband: Instead of an equal partner, he becomes another person who's your responsibility—essentially another kid. And in her research for *Drop the Ball*, Tiffany found that more financially privileged moms had a harder time letting go of household management than less-privileged and single moms. The single mothers were, by virtue of their own circumstances, more likely to look outward and utilize their community for help. (That's not to say that single mothers don't have plenty of their own shit to deal with; it's just that a useless grown man in the house you have to coddle like another child isn't necessarily part of it.)

According to the study "Marital Status and Mothers' Time Use," "both single mothers and partnered mothers spend roughly the same amount of time looking after their children. But married mothers are more likely to sacrifice their own leisure time and sleep to do unpaid housework as compared with single and divorced mothers. Researchers hypothesize that it may be tied to social expectations for women with families."

While reversing the trend of letting external pressures dictate how you live, Tiffany encourages you to take stock of your roles and reevaluate how much you put on your plate. She says to ask yourself: *What does a good wife do? What does a good mom do? What does a good manager do?* Then, look at the definitions you wrote down. Where did they come from? Chances are, you didn't simply make them up in a vacuum. Especially if you're a type A, take-charge person (*raises hand*), you may tell yourself that the pressure you feel to always have a pristine home, complete with gleaming floors and baseboards, comes from within. "If that was the case, why is it that every single woman I talk to feels *pressure* to have her home perfectly clean?" Tiffany asks. "Obviously, that was not a feeling or a decision that you made in isolation." (As a person who lives and dies by her apartment-deep-cleaning spreadsheet, that one hurts to hear.)

When it comes to Tiffany's own life, she has redefined what "good" means to her, especially after being raised by a stay-at-home mother—a "nonpaid working mom," to use her phrasing—who took care of everything for Tiffany, from cornrowing her hair to sewing her church dresses. She found herself trying to take on all of those domestic tasks *plus* maintaining her full-time job outside the home and trying to grow her career. This is where the idea of "dropping the ball" came in: Tiffany had to stop worrying about not being able to do every single thing that good moms are supposed to do, because it's already impossible. Her definition of being a good mom doesn't necessitate being present for every moment, nor does it involve keeping a picture-perfect home.

> **"I'm an incredible mom if I do three things: one, if I have an intentional conversation with my kids every day, no matter where I am, be it just over FaceTime, you know, *Who did you laugh with today? Who did you play with today? What did you learn today?* Two, my kids put scones on the list because I make really good scones, and three, my son's in the eleventh grade, so he really wanted me to help him with his ACT prep. If I do those three things, I'm a phenomenal mother. I've got my job description for all the roles that I play, and I'm just fulfilling those. I can live and be all of these things and not feel guilt."**

I'm not a parent, and this is certainly not a parenting book; I can't pass judgment on others' parenting styles or values. The point is not whether Tiffany's way is the right one. The point is that it is the right one *for her*. Your style of being a parent or wife or employee or business owner might look totally different from hers; finding fulfillment in your role simply means owning what it actually means to you.

FILL ME IN

Exercise: Redefining Your Roles

We can all afford to redefine what our roles are, even for those of us who, like myself, are not parents. Inspired by Tiffany's *"drop the ball"* philosophy, consider the various roles you play and, without thinking too much about them, write down what you associate being "good" at these roles looks like. Then, write down where that description comes from: societal expectations, social media and television, your own family, your social circles, etc. Reflect on what being good at each role actually means to you, regardless of what external influences would have you believe.

	What have you been taught being "good" looks like for this role?	Where does that definition come from?	If you could remove all external influences, what would being "good" at this role mean to you?
ROLE #1: ______ ______			
ROLE #2: ______ ______			

FILL ME IN

ROLE #3: ______ ______			
ROLE #4: ______ ______			
ROLE #5: ______ ______			
ROLE #6: ______ ______			

No, "Dropping the Ball" Is Not Devaluing Housework

A lot of this chapter has been geared toward women seeking to do less in the home so they have more energy to dedicate to the rest of their lives, and that often means work. But maybe you're not the kind of person who is driven by career ambitions, and you find you are most fulfilled when you have as much time as possible to be a present parent. Or maybe you're child-free by choice, but you also don't want to have your life dominated by your job. Any of the above are *perfectly valid*. But do not get tricked into thinking that you have to earn the right to define your own roles and set boundaries. If you're not a parent, you're still allowed to set boundaries at work, and to not take on more than your job actually requires. And I've said it before, but if you're not particularly career-driven, or if you simply earn less than your partner, *that does not mean you alone should shoulder the burden of the housework.*

But we're often trapped in exactly that dynamic, because our culture doesn't view traditionally female-coded housework in the same vein as paid labor. It's the same reason family and consumer science (aka home ec) classes are taught in schools less and less frequently: Now that seeing women in the labor force is commonplace, the time they spent in the home before doesn't count as "real work." And as I mentioned earlier, even in same-sex couples, the division of domestic labor shifts when you throw children into the mix. Since there is no clear partner who "naturally" would take on the domestic workload, typically the person earning less shoulders the majority of household labor. It's a fair trade-off, right? "I'm bringing in more money, so you should spend more time on chores."

Speaking as both the female half and the lower-earning half of a heterosexual marriage, I can tell you that's bullshit. My husband is fantastic at his job, as both an employee and a manager, but his work life isn't more stressful than mine simply because he's paid more. Of course, I'm not going to pretend there aren't nuances here, and every relationship is different. No matter how stressful my media job may feel at times, I've certainly never felt the anxiety of being an on-call firefighter or emergency room nurse, and individuals in some occupations frankly do deserve to have more time to decompress between work and household management.

Journalist Angela Garbes wrote in *The Atlantic*, "According to Oxfam, if women around the world made minimum wage for all the unpaid hours of care work they performed in 2019, they would have earned $10.8 trillion. In America alone, they would have earned $1.5 trillion, according to an analysis by *The New York Times*."

(Also, my own husband doesn't have the luxury of a four-day workweek, so yes, I often do an extra chore or two on Fridays.) Plus, plenty of people have disabilities, visible or otherwise, that keep them from being able to take on household labor in the first place; for those relationships, it of course makes sense why one partner is tackling most of the housework.

But when the same dynamic appears so frequently, the scale is generally off-balance. And when women like Tiffany "drop the ball" on domestic tasks, we shouldn't view those tasks as worthless. We should view them as important enough that they should be divided *equally* among capable members of a household, rather than putting the mental load on just one person. Unfortunately, the onus typically falls on the wife to put a change in motion when she realizes how off-balance household tasks are. When I asked Tiffany how she handled getting her husband to pick up the slack, her answer was refreshingly passive. "It's not my prerogative, really. I have enough to deal with as a woman, as a Black person, as a mom. What I really try to focus on, and the reason why my book is called *Drop the Ball*, and not 'how to get other people to pick up the ball,' is *What is within my realm of control and influence that potentially can influence the behavior and the mindsets of others?* I found that I have too much on my plate to worry about what [my husband is] doing."

According to Tiffany, many of us as women have become subjected to what she calls "home control disease"—in other words, the feeling that things must be done your way. And when you first start to drop the ball, getting over the desire to control everything can be the hardest part. There are going to be last month's Cheerios in the couch, and the mail will go unread for weeks, and the state of the baseboards will be unmentionable. But eventually, if you're in a legitimately healthy and balanced relationship, your partner will start to notice how much you really were taking on before. "You'd be surprised how quickly people learn how to vacuum," Tiffany says.

Just as this isn't a parenting book, it also isn't a relationship book. But when you are a conscientious person who is driven toward self-improvement, it can be really, *really* difficult to not take on the mental load of household management and invisible labor. Just like how people who are self-motivated to go to therapy end up continuing therapy to deal with the people in their lives who *won't* go to therapy. But that doesn't mean you should take everything upon yourself. Changing your own habits in a way that affects your entire household might start some difficult conversations, and I don't want to pretend that deep-seated behaviors we've been socialized to learn (our partners included) can be fixed with a chore division list and a household contract. But I would hope that anyone you share your life with would be open to having some frank discussions about how you divide household labor, especially once they understand how much invisible labor has been stacked on your plate, if this is an issue for you in the first place. At the end of the day, though, the only thing you can really change is your own behavior. So start there.

FILL ME IN

The Equitable Household Contract

While Tiffany's "drop the ball" philosophy is pretty aspirational, there is something to be said for setting your partner up for success. When I got married, one of the pieces of advice I heard the most was, "Don't let roommate problems become marriage problems." Now, at least in heterosexual marriages or cohabiting relationships, I think this advice should be given specifically to the man, to remind him that he is not in a relationship with his maid or his mom (gross). But many men our age simply weren't raised with the same expectations for owning household chores, so in order for things to get better, you have to meet them where they are. And that begins with an equitable household contract.

And reminder: This doesn't just apply to couples, and especially not just hetero couples! Adjust the contract for your own needs, whether you live with a partner, roommates, family members, etc. The terms of your contract will be entirely up to you, though if you need any inspiration for how to divide chores and tasks, I happily linked my own household tasks spreadsheet to the QR code at the bottom of this page. The point of making a formal-ish contract is to see this as a shared responsibility, rather than something you are *telling* them to do or *asking* them for help with. The more you can both learn to view household labor as a team effort, the less resentment there will hopefully be in the long run.

FILL ME IN

Partner #1 tasks:

Partner #2 tasks:

Shared tasks (specify exactly how they're being shared):

I, ______________________________ ("Household Partner #1"), and I, ______________________________ ("Household Partner #2"), hereby promise to take ownership of the tasks assigned to me above, including remembering, scheduling, executing, and otherwise managing each.

Signatures:

Partner #1:______________________________ Date: ______________

Partner #2:______________________________ Date: ______________

10

THE CORNER OFFICE IS ASPIRATIONAL, BUT IT'S ALSO LONELY AS HELL

We have been told that to find success as women, we need to emulate what (mainly straight/cis, white, financially privileged) men have been doing for years: ascending to the top by any means possible, then setting up camp there. But whether you're an entrepreneur, climbing the corporate ladder, or aspiring to none of the above, is a "growth at all costs" mindset *really* aspirational? For one thing, many of the girlboss CEOs who were profiled as trailblazing feminist icons have ended up stepping down over accusations of fostering a toxic work environment, practicing discrimination, and even workplace harassment. If they were trying to emulate what toxic male CEOs do, then I guess they succeeded.

According to a KPMG study, 54% of female executives agreed that they've felt lonelier the more successful they've become.

As I've explored throughout this book, the reality of chasing external validation through things like endless wealth or impressive titles is not a recipe for contentment. Yet because we've been taught to think that everyone should aspire to be a C-suite executive or an entrepreneur, we don't treat other paths as aspirational or worthy of our time. When we're only focused on ourselves and our own individual success, we lose sight of the resentments building up around us. And I can't think of a more apt example of self-driven, tunnel-vision career strategy than the Kardashian-Jenner family.

The Kardashian-Jenners: The Apex of Girlbossity

In early 2022, *Variety* released a behind-the-scenes photoshoot video with Kim and some of the other Kardashians who were doing the rounds to promote their new reality series on Hulu. And throughout the interview, they answer harmless questions about their new show, setting boundaries between real life and reality television, and their business ventures . . . and then an ill-fated question about the advice they would give to women in business, which Kim answered thusly:

> **"I have the best advice for women in business: Get your fucking ass up and work. It seems like nobody wants to work these days. You have to surround yourself with people that want to work, have a good work environment where everyone loves what they do, because you have one life. No toxic work environments, and show up and do the work."**

They all go on to talk about how important it is to be surrounded by other successful, wealthy people in order to be motivated to be more successful. Of course, that's a recipe for increased isolation and numbness to the realities of the world around you. But more to the point here is that Kim and the rest of the Kardashian-Jenner family are insulated from what hard work really looks like, because they have always had a substantial leg up. While not nepo babies in the sense that their parents weren't themselves entertainers, the Kardashian children grew up very adjacent to the industry and bolstered by enormous wealth. Kim, Kourtney, Khloé, and Rob all grew up going to private schools in one of the most elite neighborhoods in Los Angeles and landing coveted jobs as personal assistants and stylists to some of the biggest names in the early aughts (think Brandy, Paris Hilton, and Nicole Richie), all thanks to their dad's connections as an entertainment lawyer. By the time their half sisters, Kendall and Kylie Jenner, were just hitting their tween years, the family was already starring in *Keeping Up with the Kardashians*, the first of many reality shows they would go on to have.

Suffice it to say, the Kardashians and Jenners did not have an average, middle-class American upbringing. While their initial show may have started after Kim's overnight infamy from the release of her sex tape, they were ultimately given a reality show because they were a rich, attractive family—everyone's favorite kind of TV to watch. After the *Variety* video came out, writer and editor Jess DeFino wrote about her own experience working for the Kardashians' (now nonexistent) apps back in 2015, where she was paid so little while living in Los Angeles that she couldn't afford to put gas in her car:

> **"As an assistant editor, my yearly salary was $35,000—low and laughable in LA, especially considering my experience. (I wrote and produced celebrity features for outlets like *Harper's Bazaar Arabia* and *ELLE México* in my previous role at an editorial agency, but the jobs weren't steady.) *This is what it takes to work with the most famous women in the world,* I thought. . . . When the now-defunct apps launched in September 2015, featuring content I'd created over the previous five months, *The Hollywood Reporter* wrote that 600,000 people subscribed to Kylie Jenner's app alone in the first two days. *Insider* estimated the apps would generate $32,000,000 from the $3 monthly subscriptions in a single year. I was shopping for groceries at the 99 Cents Only Store."**

And the cognitive dissonance around wealth and "hard work" extends to the rest of Kim's siblings as well. When *Forbes* declared Kylie Jenner the youngest-ever "self-made billionaire" back in 2019 due to the success of her company Kylie Cosmetics, the internet was rightfully up in arms about the accolade, considering someone who was put into the reality-TV-star-to-influencer-pipeline by age ten didn't exactly have to bootstrap her way to the top. But *Forbes* initially doubled down on the distinction that she was indeed self-made because she established her fortune herself, rather than inheriting "some or all of it." And while Kylie has admitted that her already-huge platform gave her a substantial boost (as of this writing, she has the fourth-biggest Instagram account in the world, with 380 million followers), she maintains that she inherited nothing after her parents cut her off at fifteen. But as with Gwyneth Paltrow's success with Goop (and perhaps even more so), Kylie's success with her own beauty brand was a foregone conclusion. Even if she didn't inherit any literal financial assets from her insanely wealthy family, she had a built-in customer base that would take most normies a lifetime to build up. She just needed something to sell.

Of course, this all got even messier when, in 2020, it was revealed that the success of Kylie Cosmetics was largely inflated—she could no longer claim billionaire status, let alone as a self-made one. After Kylie sold 51% of her shares in the company to Coty, one of the world's largest beauty companies, *Forbes* reported that Kylie's business was both much smaller and less profitable than the Kardashians would have you believe: "*Forbes* now thinks that Kylie Jenner, even after pocketing an estimated $340 million after taxes from the sale, is not a billionaire."

Frankly, the Kardashian-Jenner family has bloated their fortune based on selling false promises to the general public for years now. I'm not going to get too in the weeds about the Kardashian family image and its implications for, you know, feminism, but it's impossible to talk about their business strategy without talking about what it is that they are marketing: a type of beauty that's impossible to achieve without spending thousands and thousands of dollars. They have made no secret about the vast fortune they've collectively spent on fillers, Botox, specialty diets, and personal trainers to look as young and conventionally attractive as possible (and that's excluding the nose jobs, BBLs, and other invasive procedures experts are pretty sure they've had over the years). Kim has Skims, a shapewear brand known as much for its bodysuits as it is for selling a "micro bikini" with coverage the size of a Dorito. Khloé has Good American, an "inclusive" denim and clothing brand that, to its credit, sells a broader range of sizes than the average American clothing

Self-Made Billionaire (n.):
a person who obtained an unethical level of wealth through the exploitation of workers and resources, typically lacking any semblance of self-awareness; an oxymoron

brand, though it still doesn't meet great standards for ethical business practices. And Kourtney has Lemme, a supplement brand selling gummies for everything from vaginal health to digestive issues.

Both Kim Kardashian's Skims and Khloé Kardashian's Good American have received a "We Avoid" rating—the lowest possible—from Good On You, a U.K.-based website dedicated to ranking brands according to ethical factors like labor conditions, animal welfare, and environmental impact.

Along with Kylie Cosmetics, those are just *some* of the companies owned by the greater Kardashian-Jenner empire. It doesn't include each sibling's other streams of income, such as dubiously disclosed sponsored content for everything from crypto to "detoxifying" teas and shakes. They will sell us literally anything to do with our own appearances, from clothing and shapewear to makeup and "nutritional" supplements, with the idea that if we just buy these things, we'll look more like them. We can buy all the thong bodysuits and lip kits we want—most of us are not going to look like a Kardashian without some serious investments in the form of lasers, fillers, and even more intense cosmetic procedures. Yet while we know their image is all smoke and mirrors, we still look at them as the apex of female success, simply because they have a lot of money.

The Problem with "Paying Your Dues"

When women like Kylie Jenner and Kim Kardashian are highlighted as self-made billionaires or publicly asked to share their advice for women in business, it reinforces the idea that these women are success stories and that their lives are something we should aspire to emulate. But what good is our understanding of success when the metric we use is the number of dollars a person (allegedly) brings in, or the number of followers they have, when they are simultaneously underpaying overworked employees and capitalizing on the detrimental beauty standards they've helped perpetuate? Is it *really* that impressive a success story when you account for the exploitation that's been integral to that success in the first place?

The Kardashian-Jenner approach to success, rooted in exploiting everything from their own public image to underpaid workers, begs the question: *Does* nobody want to work these days? Or does nobody want to be overworked and undervalued, only to not even be able to afford their groceries? The problem with career mindsets like Kim Kardashian's "get your ass up and work" mantra is that they don't *question* why no one wants to work, and especially *why no one wants to work in the ways we've been working.*

Take unpaid internships, for instance. Speaking anecdotally, I was privileged enough to be able to take more than one during my college and postgrad years, some of which even gave me useful professional experience. I'm sure some of you reading this were in the same boat. Yet most of my friends from college, at a state school where I was an out-of-state student, couldn't take the time away from their *paying* jobs in order to make room for an unpaid internship. Still, everyone I worked for in those internships and afterward held the same opinion: Being an unpaid intern was a key step in "paying your dues" and proving that you deserved to go down this particular career path. And that wasn't limited to just bootstrappy boys' club managers I worked with. Even women I interned for at a feminist magazine insisted that "kids these days" were too entitled if they thought they deserved to be paid to get their foot in the door; the experience was pay enough. (And my experience *was* good! But I should have been paid.)

I'm going to assume that most people reading this are, thank God, past the internship phase of their lives. But no matter where you stand, the reality is that unpaid internships are disproportionately taken by those who already have substantial privilege. They are a part of the system that perpetuates the myth of meritocracy, the idea that the people who succeed—such as the Kardashian-Jenner family—do so simply because they are the best, most talented, most deserving. Yet so many companies hire unpaid interns as a key step to get a foot in the door, and many all but require internship experience as a prerequisite to being hired for a paid position. In fact, 2019 data from job board site Chegg Internships showed that over 80% of employees at the Big Four consulting firms did an internship in the past, and over 70% of employees at tech companies such as Google, Facebook, and IBM did as well.

But think back to our earlier discussion of imposter syndrome. Chances are, the people you know who got early-career opportunities like unpaid internships or entry-level jobs at major corporations are not the smartest, hardest-working people you know; they are simply well-connected. The

idea of having to pay your dues a certain way is a fallacy, because the people who get those opportunities often do so through connections, familial or otherwise, with no real effort of their own. Or maybe they didn't have connections and were simply talented enough to warrant a second glance at their application, but they had family to help support them while they were doing unpaid work. Certainly not *everyone* working an unpaid internship comes from a privileged background, but many do.

According to the National Association of Colleges and Employers, 43% of internships at for-profit companies were unpaid as of 2019.

The point is that we know these systems, like unpaid internships and bloated requirements for entry-level jobs, are working in favor of a select few, and it's not fair. So when women like the Kardashian-Jenners are forming multimillion-dollar businesses and claiming to be "self-made" while paying certain employees a barely livable wage (if not less), we should not be impressed. We should not be looking to them as examples of success. And as we grow in our own careers and ascend the ladder ourselves, we should aim to be the opposite. Because when you *are* in a position of power in the workplace, it becomes more possible—and more imperative—to advocate for those coming up the ladder after you. So, if you are a manager, an entrepreneur, or in any other way in a position where you're influencing the hiring and management decisions, it's time to start thinking of ways you can use your position to positively impact the culture of your workplace.

How to Advocate Down the Ladder

When I spoke earlier about the importance of "negotiating up," I left out the opposite side of that coin: advocating down. As employees, we know what a difference a good manager can make. A good manager is willing to advocate for you, check in on you when your work seems off (rather than simply assuming you're not up to the task), and remind you to take your PTO. But know that good managers are often just as selfishly motivated as bad ones.

According to the 2022 Women in the Workplace report conducted by McKinsey and LeanIn.org, "Although more than three-quarters of White employees consider themselves allies to women of color at work, less than half take basic allyship actions, such as speaking out against bias or advocating for new opportunities for women of color."

As someone in a management role who works with a lot of creative people, the thing that makes someone stand out as an employee or contractor is not being the best or the most talented. It is being the most reliable. Having follow-through and initiating communication are *huge* assets to me, especially as someone who juggles multiple projects at once as part of her job. When employees are burnt out, their work often suffers, and they become less reliable. So I try my best to be a good manager because I care about the people who work for us, but also because *it makes my life easier.*

I think everyone, once they get to a stable enough place where they can minimize the possibility of negative consequences, should be motivated to manage well and be a workplace advocate simply because it's the kind thing to do. But I also know that people are human, and acting altruistically doesn't always come naturally. I'm highlighting the selfish reasons behind being a good manager because I'm a realist. And if we don't put the onus on managers, bosses, and other people in positions of workplace power to facilitate change, it's going to be a lot slower to happen. In a few chapters, you'll hear from Chelsea about how we started a four-day workweek at TFD and how others can advocate for that change at their own workplace. But while it has invariably meant a positive change for everyone who works there, she'll be the first to tell you that it wasn't entirely altruistic. She worked to help get us to a place where a four-day workweek was possible because *she* also wanted to work less.

According to a study from project management software company Asana, employees who experience burnout are "more likely to have lower morale (36% of people), be less engaged (30%), make more mistakes (27%) and miscommunicate (25%)."

"Advocating down" doesn't have to come only in the form of management, of course. It means looking at what you have available to you in terms of resources or how you can influence a decision, and acting on behalf of someone who is more marginalized, or less experienced, or otherwise in a position where advocating on their own behalf could have negative consequences. Here are a few direct and indirect ways to start actively advocating down:

- **Share salary budget.** If you're leading a job interview process and the interviewee quotes you a lower salary or rate than what you have budgeted for, tell them they need to ask for more (and if you can, try to make sure the job posting lists the salary). The salary negotiation gap exists in part because women, and particularly women of color, are socialized to be less confident and less assured of their value. According to data from job search site Otta, when searching for jobs, women of color enter minimum salaries that are *40% lower* than what white men put in.

* **Advocate on behalf of your reports when it is performance review time.** You know firsthand how valuable their work is; campaigning on their behalf for a raise or promotion shows them how invested you are in their growth. Also, if you know they are underpaid compared to their coworkers, or even just compared to their peers in the industry, this is your chance to help course correct.

* **Go out of your way to give positive feedback.** This also goes for people you work with but don't directly manage. If they performed really well on a project or did something to make your work life easier, tell them—and better yet, tell their direct manager or someone even higher up in the company. This can help start putting the wheels in motion to give them recognition in the form of a raise or promotion later.

* **Be open to helping train on the job.** For instance, offer to help coach a direct report or other colleague through an interview process if they are putting themself up for promotion, especially if you're familiar with what the role is and what the hiring managers are looking for.

* **Take "pick your brain" requests.** I'll be honest here: In the past couple of years, I've noticed more and more people in positions of power (especially among those working in media) sharing how they respond to informal interview requests by sending a consulting rate card. Yes, your time is valuable, and if you get a dozen requests a week, there's no reason to take them all. By all means, if some random guy you went on one bad Hinge date with messages you out

of the blue months later for free advice on his marketing strategy because he knows you work in social media, send him your rate card. But responding to a broke twenty-two-year-old looking for your advice on getting ahead in your field with a demand to be paid for your expertise is, dare I say it, rude. I'd challenge you to agree to one informal interview a month, and who knows, you might make an excellent connection from one of them! Otherwise, kindly reply with the fact that you don't have time in your schedule, and maybe forward a resource or two that might be helpful. Remember that being asked for your advice is ultimately quite flattering, and you should feel honored they're asking!

- **Set the wheels in motion for an important workplace policy change.** This could be through a comment to HR or a company-wide town hall, for instance. A friend of mine did this and it actually led to a better parental leave policy being implemented at his company! It took a while (as in, a few years), but he kept bringing it up until the decision-makers took it seriously. Be the squeaky wheel. (And let this serve as a reminder that men can, and should, be active workplace advocates, too!)

- **Stop the cycle of exploitation before it starts.** That means, if you're an entrepreneur, *don't hire an unpaid intern*. It's one thing to do a quid pro quo swap with a colleague or industry peer to get mutually beneficial services for free. It's another to continue the precedent that people should have to keep working for free in order to *potentially* level up in their careers down the line.

FILL ME IN

Becoming a Better Advocate

Those were just a few examples of advocating down. Your mileage may vary, and you have to assess what you actually have influence or control over. But if you've advanced beyond entry level and you have a good relationship with your *own* manager, your influence may be greater than you think. Below, you'll find some thought starters to identify where you can make a difference.

When was the last time you set a casual touch-base with one of your reports? Could you be more proactive about setting a recurring meeting?

When are your reports' performance reviews? Can you advocate for better pay on their behalf?

FILL ME IN

Have you made it known that you are open to opportunities to pay it forward? How so? For instance, sharing an "open call" for questions on LinkedIn.

Have you looked into joining any formal mentorship groups or programs, if you have the time and energy to devote to them?

What policies are lacking at your workplace, and how can you help start the conversation to improve them?

Unions: The Final Form of Workplace Advocacy

Of course, there is one way to be a workplace advocate that is above and beyond the rest: Help start a union.

Unions used to be much more commonplace in this country, before corporate greed and business policies of profits over people started influencing legislation in the 1970s. But that doesn't mean we can't get back to a place of better workplace policies and more equitable benefits. From Amazon to Starbucks to multiple media companies, it's been a big few years for unions in the U.S., with an increase of over 200,000 new union members in 2022.

Maybe organizing a union in your workplace is a possibility, or maybe it's not—you will be able to gauge the threat of retaliation much better than I will. The point is that unions and the benefits that came with them were once commonplace in our country, and there's no reason we can't get back to that place. And as with so much else, I'm not a union expert, but I did want to include some practical advice on starting one at your own workplace. To give us some insight, I reached out once again to Ryan Houlihan. Ryan was one of the founding members of the Bustle Digital Group Union (a contingent of the Writers Guild of America, East), which was voluntarily recognized by BDG in 2020. Here's what they had to say about what it takes to start a union, and what you can realistically expect from it.

SO YOU WANT TO START A UNION?: AN INTERVIEW WITH RYAN HOULIHAN

What is the biggest reason people should consider unionizing their workplace?

Union support is at an all-time high among Americans because studies repeatedly show that workers with unions take home more money—a lot more money. Unions are funded with a tiny percentage of that extra income, making unions one of the safest investments a worker can make. Unions can be adapted to any industry because they're designed by the very people working in that industry, which means that union members can choose to provide themselves better benefits, improved working conditions, or collective legal resources—but every union's top priority is getting their members a healthier paycheck.

What are the actual, practical steps involved in starting a union? What resources are available to those looking to start one?

There are four major steps toward forming a union. First, you want to talk amongst your coworkers and, if you haven't already, become familiar as peers. Social relationships are the key to solidarity and can give each person a better understanding of what your workplace could benefit most from. Remember, it's your protected right to discuss your working conditions or wages with fellow employees, but, in general, avoid using work devices or apps like Slack or your company's email provider to hold conversations about your workplace. Find out what your coworkers like about their jobs and what things they would change if they could. At this stage, it's okay to avoid the word "union" until you've mapped out which coworkers are most likely to be interested in formal organizing.

Second, you want to reach out for external support from an established union or union federation. Often, this means reaching out to other workers in your industry who've already unionized who can help you find the resources you'll need. The American Federation of Labor and Congress of Industrial Organizations (or AFL-CIO) is the largest federation of unions in the United States and has a wealth of experience assisting workers just like you.

Third, you and your coworkers hold discussions amongst yourselves. You'll work to formalize and streamline your communication, expand your support amongst coworkers, set your priorities, form committees, and establish an organization structure. At this point, many unions create organizing committees where people are nominated by their coworkers to leadership positions so they can more efficiently make day-to-day decisions.

Fourth, and most excitingly, you go public and request formal recognition from your employers. It's at this point that you be loud and proud about your union support to show your employer that you and your fellow union members are committed to working together to find better solutions. Your documented union support also establishes legal protections for you as a union organizer. A union is already "a union" when you form it with your coworkers. But if a union hasn't yet gotten to the negotiation table with a company, it can become "recognized" when it is certified by the National Labor Relations Board (NLRB). The NLRB is an independent federal agency that protects our right to organize. If your employer refuses to acknowledge your union, a card check can be held by the NLRB. A card check is a tally held to determine the number of signed union cards in a given workplace. If 30% of a workforce has signed a union card, an election is held. If a majority of the workforce votes in favor of unionization, the company is legally required to recognize the union and begin the bargaining process with you. From here out, your union selects a bargaining committee who regularly meets with the company's representatives and reports back to members on contract negotiations. This process can take anywhere from a few months to a few years depending on how negotiations develop. Eventually, a satisfactory contract will be reached.

What are some obstacles you faced when helping organize a union that you'd want other people to know about?

There are short-term financial incentives for executives and management to prevent workers from organizing, even when a union would strengthen the company in the long term. Because of this, company leadership can be relied upon to attempt to delay or stall workers who know they can unionize. This can result in tangible union-busting efforts and scare tactics like legal notices, misinformation campaigns, mandatory group meetings, attempts at one-on-one intimidation, future raise or benefit cuts, and anything else you can imagine. Despite high-profile attempts by Amazon, Apple, and Starbucks to test the limits of regulations, a lot of these tactics are explicitly illegal. At a company without formal pushback, you may still experience more covert union-busting tactics. At my last job, coworkers suddenly faced negative "performance" reviews, were pushed out of key responsibilities by management, and were fed misinformation through word-of-mouth campaigns. To combat these attacks, you can immunize yourself by learning your basic rights and key facts about the unionization process, which can easily debunk lies before they can get any lift. It's also important for workers to regularly check in with each other about what they are experiencing, document all their interactions with management, and stand in solidarity when their coworkers make factual observations or statements about their workplace that an employer may not want to recognize. This is also where outside organizations like the NLRB, AFL-CIO, or a union similar to your own can lend legal resources and expertise.

Realistically, what can people expect having a union in place at work to fix for them? What is beyond the control of a union?

A union is an organized and protected way to improve your collective employment contract, not a magic wand. A union can provide a ton of benefits that workers are desperate for—health benefits, vacation time, safety equipment, legal resources, mutual aid, and more. Truly, the list can match any ambitions you and your coworkers can dream up. Unions, like any organization, should be built to be antidiscriminatory from their very inception, and protections need to be put in place at every stage of the organizing process to ensure equity. Unfortunately, there will always be situations in which human beings fail. A union can't suddenly make everyone in your workplace ethical or kind, but it does establish a safer and more impactful way to address your issues than raising them with management at an employer deeply invested in the status quo.

11

KILLING YOUR INNER GIRLBOSS AND RECLAIMING YOUR ACTUAL LIFE

Ever since I started working at TFD, we have been campaigning in favor of the anti–dream job agenda, because the perfect dream job simply doesn't exist in real life. Even if you're one of the lucky ones who gets to do work that you find creatively or emotionally fulfilling, it's still going to feel like work *most of the time*. It doesn't matter if you have the coolest job title in the world; no one is going to spend hours of each day chasing inbox zero and trying to get ahold of Sharon from accounting and think, *Wow, I'm really living the dream*. Unfortunately, for those of us who were socialized into thinking that your job is the ultimate expression of your identity, we've collectively cornered ourselves into habits we can't break. And that means that, beyond the toxicity of the only-look-out-for-yourself mentality, there's another side effect of living a hashtag-girlboss, hustle-at-all-costs lifestyle: working so much that you literally don't have time for your actual life.

The pandemic exacerbated our tendency to overwork ourselves. In 2022, 55% of PTO went unused on average, compared to just 28% in 2019, the year before the world shut down. And it's worse for lower-rung workers; compared to high earners, lower earners who have PTO use 52% less of it.

The fact that we can't unplug from the Matrix (by, you know, logging off at a reasonable hour, or using all our PTO) isn't our fault. When we say we want better work-life balance, companies start "wellness initiatives" with the expectation that a free membership to a meditation app and a 10% discount to Equinox will keep us happy. But that's not good enough.

There are things you can start doing *now* to divorce yourself from your tendency to overwork and form long-term habits to protect yourself from burnout.

The Inevitable Link Between Busyness and Burnout

Everyone has that one friend who just won't shut up about how unbelievably busy they are. You'll ask a simple "How are you doing?" only to be met with a tirade of complaints: the client who's taking up all their time, the meetings they had to sit through today, the fact that they haven't been able to even passively watch TV in over a month. They brag about having gone five years without once taking a sick day. Often, it's not that they're actually busier than anyone else. They have just internalized a pervasive message we can't seem to escape: that busyness is a virtue.

When interviewed in an article for *Vice* titled "The Cult of Busyness," Jonathan Gershuny, co-director of the Center for Time Use Research, said, "Just as being leisurely around 1900 was a status claim, being unmanageably busy at the turn of this century was a status claim based on the fact that the busiest people also tended to be the richest." These days, rich people don't squander their money and time on leisure the way their counterparts born centuries ago would have, i.e., gallivanting around gambling halls and brothels like a rake in a romance novel. Having wealth used to be a reason to work less, but now, professional success is just as much of a class marker as money. For many who belong to the 1%, it doesn't matter how much money they have already made, or that they can afford to retire a thousand times over—they often have some new venture they're funding, some new start-up they're launching. Billionaire tech bros like Elon Musk and Mark Zuckerberg and businesswomen like the Kardashians are the new, and more intense, landed aristocracy. And when you grow up being taught to chase a meaningful "dream job" above all else, you try to at least mimic that busyness. Your work may be dull, and you may be underpaid, but by allowing it to keep you as busy as possible, at least you're emulating those guys. That proves you're worth something, right?

I spoke with Eve Rodsky, author of *Find Your Unicorn Space: Reclaim Your Creative Life in a Too-Busy World*, about our obsession with being busy and why it's a problem for so many. In her research, she's found that two of the most common words people use to describe their lives are "mundane" and "overwhelm." "Because we only give people two choices for how to live right now in a burnout culture, overwhelm and mundane, people often latch on to the overwhelm," she said. "And it's really not their fault. But it sort of becomes a badge of honor, because we really don't know a way out."

And the culture of overworking extends to creative "dream jobs" as well. Ingrid Nilsen was, by all metrics, an incredibly successful YouTuber for over ten years, with more than 3.5 million subscribers and dozens of videos surpassing the million-view mark. But by 2020 (a few months into the pandemic), she'd had enough. "I wasn't getting what I wanted out of that career anymore," she told me. "I felt like I had given what I had to give creatively, mentally, emotionally, and it just felt like in every part of my body that it was time to stop." I asked her what it was about content creation as a career that excessively lent itself to burnout, and here's what she had to say:

> **"I have yet to see a long-term sustainable way to just keep going with content creation, because it puts so much burden on one human being . . . you have your niche, and then you feel like you have to stay in that niche and just repeat the same thing over and over again. And then if you start making money, then you feel the pressure to *keep* doing so, especially if you have a team of people who are working for you. There is this pressure to keep doing more."**

For Ingrid, and arguably many creators like her who've left YouTube and other platforms, that pressure eventually led to her taking a step down and starting a different career path. For many, many others, it led to the most talked-about workplace trend of the early 2020s: quiet quitting.

Quiet Quitting: The Inevitable Consequence of Busyness

In the past few years, "quiet quitting" has been covered by every single mainstream media platform. It's a response to the collective realization that taking on more at work is not, in fact, a direct path to a lucrative career or a fulfilling life. An article in *The Atlantic* called it a "fake trend," claiming it "might stand in for chronic labor issues such as the underrepresentation of unions or a profound American pressure to be careerist." But while it's perhaps been given an overly simplified, reactive name, quiet quitting is far from made up.

A 2022 Gallup poll found that the ratio of engaged to disengaged employees was 1.8 to 1—the lowest in nearly a decade.

Per my previous chapter and the reality of being underpaid and undervalued while expected to do the most, it makes sense that we would start to quiet quit en masse. Unfortunately, it's not really a long-term solution to burnout, especially if you face consequences (legal or otherwise) at work. For one thing, think about the expectation you set when you're known to always go above and beyond, or when you're the first one online and the last to log off. If you try to randomly put boundaries in place where they didn't previously exist, it's likely going to be perceived as slacking off—and that could lead to a negative performance review, or worse.

It's much easier to start from zero and never set the expectation that you're willing to overwork yourself in the first place. But walking away from a job when you're inclined to quiet quit doesn't *have* to be the answer. First, try talking to your manager about your situation. If they're not receptive to figuring out how to cut down your overwhelming to-do list because you're a real-life human being, appeal to them from a business perspective. When I spoke with Tiffany Dufu, she said dropping the ball at work is just as imperative as doing so at home—but you have to navigate the situation carefully. Here's her short script that anyone can tailor to their own conversations with management:

> **"One of the observations I've made is that whenever I'm really front-facing with the client, I can move through the pipeline and close deals. But one of my other observations is that that's not where I'm spending the majority of my time. I'm spending the majority of my time uploading data into the database, and I'm wondering if you're open to a conversation about how we might be able to provide a leadership opportunity to someone else on the team to take that over so I can spend more of my time with the client, and ensuring that we nail this quarter. Are you open to that conversation?"**

Of course, the better the relationship you have with your manager in the first place, the better this will go over. The goal is to get yourself to a place where you are spending work hours only on what's in your actual job description, without sabotaging your position in the company.

Sometimes, though, quiet quitting can be symptomatic of a larger issue in your professional life. If you work somewhere with a toxic overworking culture, the best option may be to look for a job elsewhere. But sometimes, the very industry you find yourself in is the problem. In order to get a glimpse into what it looks like to make a drastic career change *without* landing yourself in the same burnt-out condition as before, I spoke at length with Ingrid Nilsen about the process of starting her candle company, The New Savant. Ingrid was, of course, in a very privileged financial position to be able to take a long break from her career and start a whole new work chapter. But I think anyone can gain some valuable insight from her about creating a job that's not your whole life, and choosing stability and sustainability over growth at all costs.

THE LATERAL CAREER LEAP: AN INTERVIEW WITH INGRID NILSEN

What made you decide to start The New Savant?

After I quit YouTube, I gave myself my first real break in over a decade. I had $566,000 in savings. So I knew I had some time to just hang out and take a break, but I also knew that I didn't have money to just live forever without working again.

It was in August of 2020 [when my co-founder Erica and I were visiting her dad in Indiana], and I saw a candle, and I thought to myself, *Oh, I wonder how candles are made.* And then I thought, *I bet I could figure it out.* So I went to the craft store and brought the supplies back and made my first candles on Erica's childhood ping-pong table and was just completely enamored by the process.

It became clear to me that I was *okay* creatively turning this into a business. It's that sweet spot of, *I enjoy this creatively; I feel like I'm being challenged; I feel like there is a lot of open space in the fragrance world, and I feel like I can contribute in a meaningful way.* So I reached out to different suppliers, and I asked Erica if she wanted to get on board and help me with the business side of things and help me launch. I made my first candles in my kitchen, and we launched with about 500 candles and sold out in seven minutes in December 2020.

What intentional choices did you make when it came to using your platform to promote this new brand?

I used about one-eighth of the platform that I had. I mentioned it in passing on Instagram but didn't utilize my YouTube or any of my other social media platforms. Of course, there were people who knew me from my YouTube days who came over, and that really gave us a leg up in terms of awareness. The challenge became, *how do you keep it going?* And that's when I think I really learned a lot from Erica and really leaned on her, because she is someone who, when she has a question about something, she'll reach out to people that she knows, even if she doesn't talk to them regularly, and just ask questions.

What's been your strategy for growth? Have you felt the pressure to take on outside money?

I have invested about $30,000 of my own money into the business over time, because we do have to buy supplies in order to make our product. But I really didn't want to take on [investors too early]. I've just seen the stress that other founders have gone through that have taken on a lot of money; a lot of times, it's almost like you have too much money too soon, and then you start doing all these things that don't actually make sense, but you just have to spend the money.

By being self-funded up to this point, we're very able to see where our pain points are. Flexibility was also really important to me when starting a business. I wanted to be able to make quick changes if we needed to, and not have to ask somebody about it, and make creative decisions that I wanted to make, because we are building a fragrance company that's different. We're creating scent profiles that are outside of the white, Eurocentric, French-man-perfumer world. But we have built a profitable business, and we want to keep it that way. We don't want to be in the hole and scrambling to try to make up this money that we have taken on. It's allowed us to build a customer base that is extremely, extremely loyal.

Have you approached the same level of burnout that you experienced with YouTube?

I don't feel like I'm approaching that level of burnout, and I think it's because I have done a lot of work personally, figuring out how I want to feel, how I work creatively. . . . There are challenges with running a business, but that's a given. I didn't start this because I thought it was going to be easy. I'm happy because this is fun. I'm happy because I'm creatively fulfilled. And I also stop at 4:45, and I go to a Pilates class four or five days out of the week. I just don't have the anxiety that I had while I was making content, and I think it's because my goal in life was not to be the product.

FILL ME IN

Exercise: A Work-Life Audit

When you feel like you're in a professional rut, it can be difficult to identify what your next move should be. It could just be that you're knee-deep in a busy season, and this chaotic period will pass. Or it could mean you're under a manager or in a workplace with a culture that doesn't align with your values, and you need to move departments, or even companies, or industries.

First, perform a full audit of your work life, and list out all of your responsibilities and regular tasks. If you're having issues identifying your work tasks, refer to the time audit spreadsheet on page 149 to start tracking how you spend your work hours.	
Are you currently taking on an excess of tasks that don't fall under your job description? List them here.	
If the above tasks are taking up a substantial amount of your working hours, it might be time to have a candid conversation with your manager. Do you feel comfortable voicing issues at your current workplace? Why or why not?	

FILL ME IN

Which of the major tasks from your time audit do you enjoy? Which do you not enjoy?	
Refer to your list of core values on pages 46–47—does your current work life align with your values? For instance, if you've identified that you prioritize flexibility, does your job allow for that?	
Is it possible to make the changes you need to make in your current job, company, or industry? Or do you need a bigger career change?	

Curing Your Burnout: Playing the Long Game

At the end of the day, fixing your relationship with your job is only one-half of creating a sustainable plan to combat burnout. When you put in the effort to make your job fit your life, and not the other way around, you must decide what to do with that extra time. Eve Rodsky spent a long time researching this, and she found that while people expect burnout to be fixed with simple self-care or a yearly girls' trip, the answer is a lot more complicated. "Friendships are so important, and so is self-care—not commodified wellness, but true self-care," she said. "But the truth is, the antidote to burnout is being consistently interested in your own life, and that's a harder message to sell people. I can't give you a supplement that will fix everything."

So how do you start taking a real interest in your own life? Contrary to our earlier discussion of the problem with glorifying busyness, Eve doesn't actually see anything wrong with being busy. The problem is *why* you're busy.

> **"So many women have said to me that they're *allowed* to be busy as parents, they're *allowed* to be busy as partners supporting their partner, and they're *allowed* to be busy as professionals. But God forbid you're busy as an amateur gymnast at night, or you want to tell your boss right at five o'clock you're going to take your mixology class. Like you're not allowed to be busy with those things."**

But filling your schedule with "values-based pursuits," aka unicorn spaces, is the key to staving off burnout. These are activities that a) spark your curiosity, b) involve connection, meaning they aren't solo activities, and c) have an element of completion, so you're motivated to keep going. Your own anti-burnout outlet could be any number of things. One of Eve's favorite examples to point to is a woman living in Queens who decided to join a "polar bear plunge" group, where every weekend they jumped into the freezing cold Atlantic Ocean. "My challenge to people is to do something where you come out of it and say, 'I can't believe I just did that,'" like that woman must have the first time she jumped in the frigid water. (Could not be me but love that journey for her.)

> **"I call it 'unicorn space' because like the magical equine, it doesn't fucking exist until you reclaim it; we're still conditioned to be just parents, partners, and professionals on repeat. But the beauty of these pursuits is often they're even less expensive than the hedonistic pursuits that take over our lives. Binge watching, having seventeen different subscriptions to, like, Netflix and HBO, edibles, or fine wines . . . not that they're bad, but I see many women telling me that they're numbing themselves through their lives. Whereas your values-based busyness ends up being less expensive monetarily, and better for your soul, better for your mental health."**

Unicorn spaces can be hobbies—as long as they aren't completely solitary ones (though it's great to have those, too!). And while I've never put a name to it, I definitely have embraced the importance of these spaces in my own life. Last year I took weekly ice skating classes, and this year I finally started indoor rock climbing—something I'd been wanting to try, and finally worked up the courage thanks to my husband and a few friends who wanted to do the same. Without realizing it, my husband has his own unicorn spaces, too; he has biweekly piano lessons where he's learning to arrange music, and he also joined a Dungeons & Dragons campaign. (You can pick your partner, but you can't pick your partner's interests.) The point is not to say that you prioritize your own creative outlets *over* your family, friends, and work life; rather, it's to prioritize your own interests *as much as* you prioritize everything else in life. "It's not optional," Eve says. "Having these values-based pursuits doesn't take away the overwhelm and mundane [of life]. It's going to rain on you—but they give you an umbrella."

FILL ME IN

Exercise: Planning Your Anti-Burnout Outlet

Using the parameters that Eve set forth, use this space to brainstorm an anti-burnout outlet. Remember, this will need to be something that gets you out of the house (at least some of the time), fits within your core values, sparks your curiosity, and involves interacting with others. For example, if you value physical activity and healthy competition, you could join a pickleball league. If you value cultural experiences and lifelong learning, your outlet could be learning Spanish with a group or tutor—better yet, joining a Spanish-practice meetup group in your area. If you value healthy debate and creating community, you could start or join a book club.

Think back to your core values and list your top three here:

Brainstorm five anti-burnout activities. Which one appeals to you the most?

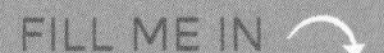

Is it something you can start immediately, or will it take some planning? (Either is fine—just start planning ahead for it!)

What costs will you incur by doing this activity? Can you make space for it in your current "id" spending?

What time commitment will this involve? How will you plan to make space for it in your schedule?

List the steps you can take to start putting this plan into action:

This week:

This month:

This quarter:

12

THE 40-HOUR WORKWEEK AND OTHER TOXIC MYTHS

By Chelsea Fagan,
CEO of The Financial Diet

There was a time when computers felt like the dawn of a glorious era of freedom. There were going to be these machines, then the size of rooms, but one day small enough to fit in our pockets, and they were going to do all of our work for us. We wouldn't have to manually figure out long, tedious math problems. We wouldn't want to throw our typewriters out the window in a blind rage when we made a single mistake on an important correspondence. We wouldn't have to strap that correspondence to the leg of a pigeon and hope it reaches its destination in a reasonable amount of time—these little machines would do all of that for us. And the philosophers and idealists, the tech maximalists, had good reason to believe that such an unprecedented level of synthesis between human ingenuity and machine efficiency would be the beginning of the end of hard work, with some even predicting a fifteen-hour week by this time in history. What they couldn't account for, unfortunately, were the Boybosses of Late Capitalism, ready to transmute any technological progress into depressing obligation.

It simply didn't occur to them that, rather than greatly reducing the raw hours it would take to complete a task by utilizing computers, the constant presence of communication-ready technology would mean expanding the "workplace" into a limitless horizon that now occupied your home, your bedroom, your commute, your vacations, and even your increasingly anxiety-riddled dreams. Because now there is never a valid excuse of "not being at your desk," there is never a reason to not be available to work. (We can see a similar sleight of hand with the supposed liberation of remote work: That arduous commute time many people have finally reclaimed has in many cases been absorbed into expected working hours, because it was never perceived as theirs to begin with.) Simply put, the computer has served to turn many employers into all-reaching panopticons, the job-central locus of your life, where a push notification is always waiting to jump-scare you out of whatever you dared to be enjoying at that moment.

And similarly, though this world-historic level of efficiency did indeed translate to a vastly increased productivity, the shareholder value—

driven model of our economy all but guaranteed that none of the spoils would filter down to the workers actually responsible for them. Wages have stagnated over the same decades during which what we created increased, leading to an ever-separating relationship between "what we are worth" and "what we receive." In some ways, that techno-idealist vision of a world where computers mean value that spirals infinitely upward while the actual labor required to realize it becomes more passive was true. It just applies to the capital-owning class, who has seen their wealth increase exponentially while living conditions get worse for nearly everyone else on the economic ladder.

In some ways, though, the most depressing part of all of this is just how normalized these dynamics have become for the people they impact the most negatively. We have vastly increased the available workforce by driving women into the workplace—once a liberatory act, now a financial necessity, regardless of preference—therefore further depressing the value of labor and increasing workplace redundancy. Though by every metric we should be working less, it has become not just a status symbol but a moral imperative to work more, to identify yourself with your job first and foremost, and to demonstrate your worthiness through working increasingly long hours—a rather Calvinist notion. As the author Anne Helen Petersen put it in her excellent book on burnout, *Can't Even:*

> **"When people follow a 'calling,' money and compensation are positioned as secondary. The very idea of a 'calling' stems from the early precepts of Protestantism and the notion that every man can and should find a job through which they can best serve God. American Calvinists interpreted dedication to one's calling—and the wealth and success that followed—as evidence of one's status as elect. This interpretation was conducive to capitalism, the cultural theorist Max Weber argues, as it encouraged every worker to see their labor not just as broadly meaningful, but worthwhile, even sacred."**

The data that shows that the wealthy tend to work more than average is sometimes misinterpreted as evidence that they are creating more value or are more deserving of their outsize compensation. But the truth is that it points to a much greater sickness of the American soul: a constant need to justify and prove oneself through association with work, an addiction to the aesthetics of being busy, the abstract value of obscene executive bonuses and compensation packages (and CEO compensation, in particular) that are more about the increasing number than the additional potential luxury they represent for the recipient.

Put simply, the less we needed to work, the more we began to associate ourselves with our careers. Through the always watchful eyes of the smartphone and laptop, work has gone from being an inconvenient means to an end to an identity of its own. And with labor organizing more suppressed and weakened than it's nearly ever been (though there are a few heartening examples in recent years of its resurgence), we have lost the language with which to advocate for what always should have been rightfully ours. All workers deserve to see the technological dream come true. We deserve to see the spoils of our blinding productivity and work ethic. We deserve to reclaim vast swaths of our lives.

And for myself, as CEO of my small-but-mighty company, I am constantly thinking about how we can better achieve that ourselves. Once we were no longer bound by the day-to-day pressure of paying our bills—a constant slow-drip anxiety that impedes your ability to consider anything beyond the number in the company's bank account—we had to decide what it actually means to live well with the work we're doing. There was the relatively low-hanging fruit, like assuring that all our employees were compensated at a certain level and engaged in at least some kind of profit sharing. We also moved from the false promise of "unlimited PTO" (a system I'd experienced at previous employers and automatically assumed at TFD but came to regret, as it demonstrably results in employees actually taking less time off) to a healthy six weeks of PTO for each full-time staffer. We were starting to embrace a work-life balance that put profit on the backburner but kept employee retention near 100%, resulted in increased productivity and satisfaction, and improved the quality of work we were doing at every level.

But then came the less obvious but, in my opinion, even more necessary question: Do we even need to work that much? We'd already engaged in summer Fridays for several years, and there was nothing special about the months between Memorial Day and Labor Day that allowed us to suddenly increase our brain capacity or typing speed to match our regular output despite leaving at noon one day of each week. Why not try doing "summer Fridays" year-round and see if the results stuck? Or maybe, my colleague posited when we were initially laying out our four-day workweek experiment, we should try just doing away with an entire day of work and see if we're able to achieve the results we want. The four-day workweek had been attempted and embraced by an increasing number of organizations larger and more complex than ours; it seemed sensible that the streamlined nature of our already lean team would lend itself to an even nimbler structure.

Two years later, we have turned our four-day workweek experiment into a mode of being for our company. Without lowering salaries or benefits, we simply started working eight fewer hours each week and have never looked back. We internally refer to the concept as our thirty-two-hour workweek, as sometimes we find ourselves logging on for a bit on Fridays, or working in the evenings when we have an event, then taking the following morning to ourselves. With a deliverable-based definition of success, it simply doesn't matter when or how the work gets done; it only matters that we're able to do it. There is no need to continually be filling our days with work, or the

Unlimited PTO (n.):
a clever sleight of hand adopted by employers, especially in the tech and start-up spaces, to give the illusion of ample work-life balance without ever actually committing to providing it

illusion of work, because we're stuck at our desks and need to make use of the time. We have our objectives, we have our metrics of success, and once we meet them, the hours are ours to reclaim.

There were a few key factors in making our experiment successful, and they boiled down to sussing out with the accuracy of a surgeon's scalpel exactly where the value lay in the work we were doing, and where we were only pantomiming the rituals of a typical white-collar job. For us, that meant that a few key areas needed a serious reckoning:

- **Meetings:** While sometimes necessary and arguably even often effective, they are an invasive species to the ecosystem of actually doing meaningful, thoughtful work. Where we had hour-long meetings, they were trimmed to thirty minutes. Where we had thirty-minute meetings, they were halved to a quarter of an hour. The tiny stand-ups were often transferred to Slack or email, where the fluffy formalities of jargon and small talk wouldn't need to bog down the otherwise straightforward exchange of relevant information.

- **Delegation:** Sometimes a task is by necessity a shared one and benefits from the collaborative outcome of multiple perspectives. However, we often make projects more collaborative than necessary, at best causing a slower and more redundant process, and at worst leading to the familiar morass of no one actually taking ownership. In an effort to preserve everyone's time, delegation of exactly who is responsible for what became more crucial than ever before.

- **Flexibility:** Partially due to the pandemic, we went from a workplace that was mostly in-office to one that is 50% work from home. We are a friendly, chatty team that enjoys one another's company, but we are also human beings with full lives that benefit immensely from two days per week without a commute or distraction, and a three-day weekend each week. Allowing plentiful WFH time means heightened concentration and productivity, particularly because we generally try not to schedule any internal meetings on the days we're not in the office. Our time is ours to reclaim and maximize.

- **Socialization:** While we were never the ultra-social kind of company, the pressure to fraternize with coworkers outside of work hours is something we actively try to minimize. A company is not a family, the workplace shouldn't be your social circle, and hanging out constantly with other employees is just a way to further blur the lines of when you

> are and aren't at work. If two colleagues want to hang out, great, but it shouldn't be a requirement of the job, and it absolutely should not contribute to an already immense social pressure to consume alcohol. Our team-wide hangs occur a few times a year, usually at lunches (and therefore during work hours) and are friendly to all types of revelers.

In many ways, the adjustments we made to ensure that a four-day workweek was sustainable were the corrections that nearly every professional job is in dire need of, regardless of working hours. Meetings are overused, the appearance of work rather than its outcome is often prioritized, the environment is too heavily constrained, and the pressure to make your work into your life is all but inescapable. These philosophies of better work didn't just make the experiment a success (though they did, as our profitability, productivity, and employee satisfaction all increased substantially): They made us a better organization. We are now that much closer to living the ethos we discuss on our platforms.

Whether it pertains to personal finance or professional success, the most life-altering shift one can make is realizing when enough is enough. You can earn unfathomable sums of money and still live paycheck to paycheck if your lifestyle inflation outpaces your salary. And you can annex greater and greater swaths of your personal life for your career while never becoming any better or more creative at your job. In both cases, the constant spiraling toward more is the thing that condemns us to dissatisfaction and to an obsession with means at the expense of the ends. We have tricked ourselves into thinking that working long hours, week after week, proves that our work is important or that we are great at what we do. In reality, it only demonstrates our inefficiency and our employers' inability to truly value their teams. It's similar to constantly spending at the top of our means instead of knowing when we have enough: It keeps us trapped in a feedback loop of inadequacy.

I understand that enacting this four-day workweek experiment at every employer will be an uphill battle, and that it will require more of a fundamental shift in some industries than others—in many cases, a revolution in staffing so that the overlong hours that have become normalized in some spaces are no longer necessary. But it's an endeavor worth attempting.

As Holly has already discussed in this book, the higher up you are in an organization, the more of an ethical responsibility you have to advocate for these things. It's not just that you are more likely to be able to implement such changes, or to convince those who can. It's also that company cultures, unlike the American economy, actually operate in a trickle-down manner. The unhealthy habits that calcify at the top of corporate ladders (always being reachable by email, expecting unrealistic turnarounds, filling calendars with unnecessary or overlong meetings) become the norms by which everyone else must live. If you are a manager, if you lead teams, it's your job to demonstrate not just what good work looks like, but how it gets done, starting with structuring your work in such a way that it doesn't cannibalize your life.

The most important thing to understand when advocating for a four-day workweek, especially to old-school executives—who are often as resistant to change as they are to the concept that they could be wrong—is that it *works*. In most white-collar jobs, the actual amount of necessary work that gets done in an average forty-hour week takes far less time than those forty hours. Most of us are already engaging in redundant tasks, or involved in projects for which we are not necessary, or spending time just staring at our screens in an approximation of thoughtfulness. The key is demonstrating that we don't need as much time as we think we do, and that switching to a more streamlined way of working reduces the mental load on employees, increases their creativity and ability to produce, and skyrockets their retention. Executives may not listen to arguments about their humanity or the glittering potential of their lives outside of work, but they will listen to increased profit margins or reduced turnover, both of which the four-day workweek has strong arguments for.

On page 223 we've included a little presentation you can show your higher-ups to get the ball rolling on this experiment at your own company, possibly starting it in the summer when many organizations already implement some kind of relaxed working schedule. As with anything in work, the idea is to present this as a net positive for the company, on the terms the company prioritizes. While I (and hopefully you) believe that making these kinds of changes is important for our economy, our culture, and our collective mental health, it's important to speak the language of those we want to reach. So our outline here is a guide to making those arguments from a data-driven, profit-minded perspective so they will be received well and have a chance of actually being implemented.

There is nothing magical about our company, nothing we inherently know better or do more optimally than many other small businesses that folded in the near decade we've been able to thrive. If anything, our secret formula is our lack of adherence to the identity that work often creates, especially in small, tight-knit teams. In doing a survey of our staff, my colleague found that they actually identified slightly less with the statement "I am proud to work for this company" after a year of the four-day workweek. While superficially this may seem like a negative for an organization, both she and I actually regard it as a wonderful thing. It's also a sentiment I share personally. In the time since we've begun the experiment, our staff have become mothers, bought homes, started side projects, gotten married, traveled the world, and done a hundred other things that are equally or more valuable to the work they do with our company, myself included. We are less tied to the satisfaction and validation that the work gives us because it simply takes up less real estate in our lives and in our minds. We are many things, and the person we are at work is one of them, but it's certainly not the totality, or even the majority, of who we are. We contain multitudes and give our best to our work at The Financial Diet for the hours we dedicate to it each week, but we don't live and die by its progress.

You contain multitudes, too. You deserve to enjoy a life that is rich and diverse and fulfilling in so many ways beyond whatever professional accolades you accumulate. You can be great at your job without giving yourself over to it, and I would argue—as would the data about these experiments—that you're actually much better at your job when it represents less of your life. You get to arrive at work refreshed and relaxed, eager to give it your all because you know that you'll be able to set it aside comfortably in a few days. You get to enjoy life, rather than just find a means to pay for it.

FILL ME IN

Presenting Your Own Four-Day Workweek

Below, you will find a QR code linking to a slideshow template we've created to demonstrate what a four-day workweek proposal could look like—simply make your own copy to edit. Remember that the most important thing is to frame the four-day workweek in a way that benefits your employer specifically—because while we'd love to think they'd be over-the-moon ecstatic to make their employees' lives better, we're not wishful thinkers.

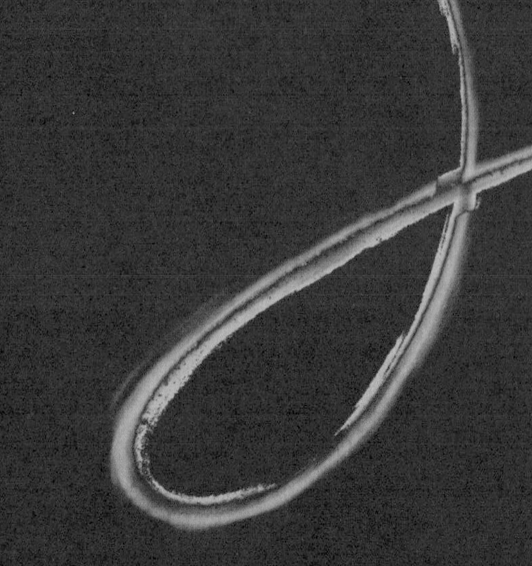

13

DITCHING INTERNET SELF-CARE AND EMBRACING INCONVENIENCE

I feel like I have spent this entire book throwing contradictions at you. *Don't overthink your budget, but plan ahead for your just-for-fun spending. Don't let lifestyle inflation back you into a financial corner, but don't spend too cheaply, either. Don't lose sight of the systemic issues that are preventing so many from living fulfilling lives, but don't stop working toward a better quality of life for yourself. Don't squander your life on work and nothing else, but make sure you're facilitating what you're worth. Don't forget to advocate for yourself, but advocate for those coming up the ladder behind you, too.*

But if I have learned anything from all my years spent talking to strangers on the internet about money, it's that living a fulfilling life is entirely about balance. It's working toward that promotion that will give you more freedom to take the family vacation. It's spending less on cheap clothes you'll wear once so you can spend more on that one piece you'll cherish forever. It's taking care of yourself so you have more to give back to others. Embracing contradictions—rather than fighting against them—is the only way to end up feeling in control of your own life, at least for most of us. And that's a difficult message to sell.

We exist in a culture and a media landscape that glamorize quick fixes over cultivating long-term habits that can legitimately change our lives in the long run—because the quick fixes are easier. "Ten ways to save a thousand dollars right now" is always going to get more clicks than "how to take care of your financial future while also enjoying the present." Monthlong challenges like the Whole30 diet and dry January promise to help people reset their bodies with extreme measures,

> **The Quick-Fix Industrial Complex (n.):** how the media has tricked us into thinking the key to having the life, body, and bank account we want is a series of five-minute hacks and thirty-day challenges

even though many of us could make moderate lifestyle tweaks that make a huge difference (but only as long as we stick to them). And it's always important to remember who is selling us on these quick fixes. Those personal trainer fitfluencers who share thirty-second TikToks with titles like "a total-body workout to get you looking snatched in fifteen minutes" tend to conveniently leave out the fact that you'd have to repeat it most days for *months* in order to actually see results, and also, they probably became a personal trainer because they were already genetically blessed with conventional good looks and a metabolism they didn't have to work for.

Unfortunately, since we do tend to focus on quick fixes, life hacks, and instant gratification, we lose sight of the habits that *would* make us better off in the long run. And one harmful iteration of this is how we are torpedoing our social well-being in the name of "setting boundaries."

The Evolution of Boundary Setting

Setting boundaries in the name of self-care is not a new topic. It was a mainstream discussion by the time I started at TFD in 2016—making me basically middle-aged in internet years. There are entire social media accounts dedicated to setting boundaries within your relationships, friendships, and work life. Many are run by licensed mental health professionals; many more are not. They have evolved from text-based Instagram graphics to thirty-second TikTok explainers, but the content itself hasn't changed much. Boundaries are crucial for protecting your mental health, from preventing codependency in a relationship to not letting your life be consumed by work.

"I think back to when I was in grad school, and there was very little talk about boundaries," said Maria Sosa, a licensed marriage and family therapist. She'd learned about boundaries from a specific therapeutic standpoint in school but didn't spend too much time on it. But when she started creating and sharing mental health content on social media, the idea of setting boundaries was blowing up. "It was everywhere. You couldn't go anywhere without hearing people talk about boundaries or creating content about boundaries or knowing what boundaries were." She also said, of course, having access to so much mental health advice was new for so many people, thanks to social media.

> **"I don't think everybody had access to as much wealth of information, especially not from therapists who are trained in dealing with boundaries and relationships and family dynamics. I think it's just so readily accessible, and a lot of the time free, that individuals have really bought into the idea of [setting boundaries] and want to incorporate it into their lives."**

With the way hustle culture has fostered our obsession with work and productivity, a revolution in the name of setting boundaries was a foregone conclusion. Author and minister Tricia Hersey captured it aptly in her book *Rest Is Resistance:* "Capitalism has cornered us in such a way that we can only comprehend two options. 1: Work at a machine level, from a disconnected and exhausted place, or 2: Make space for rest and space to connect with our highest selves while fearing how we will eat and live." And as we've seen with the evolution of the idea of "having it all," women especially are socialized to put others before themselves.

In a survey of 1,000 Americans conducted by market research company YouGov, 56% of women would "definitely" describe themselves as people pleasers, compared to just 42% of men.

The message "protect your peace" has been popularized, particularly among Black women, as a response to the toll and tiredness that result from always having to tough it out in a society that undervalues you. For many, including many queer and trans individuals and others who may face intolerance even from those they're supposed to be closest to, protecting your peace can mean cutting ties with toxic family members or former friends, or situations that can put you in harm's way. Boundaries can play a crucial role not only in people's mental health but also in their physical safety.

When Boundaries Don't Fix Your Problems

But somewhere along the way, the ultimate message of how to set boundaries for the benefit of your health got lost in translation. Instagram-influenced FOMO turned into JOMO, the joy of missing out. Under the hashtag #protectyourenergy on Instagram, every other result on the first page is a sincere listicle of how to stop giving your energy to things that aren't serving you, followed by a meme that says, "When you find out your normal daily lifestyle is called 'quarantine'" or "What makes life so difficult? People." When I idly scroll through TikTok before bed (no, I'm not perfect, but is that a crime?), it feels like every other video is a joke about the relief of having social plans canceled at the last minute. And for those of us who remember the introvert industrial complex that took over Tumblr in the 2010s, this messaging isn't anything new, nor is it going anywhere, though maybe there will be new platforms sucking up our mental energy beyond Instagram and TikTok by the time this book is published. "Setting boundaries" was a key component of resistance and self-care, but it has been co-opted to become a catchall excuse to avoid doing anything mildly inconvenient in favor of chilling on the couch with a face mask, popcorn, and a sixth rewatch of *Bridgerton*, season two.

Anyone can, and should, set the boundaries they need to protect their mental, emotional, and often physical well-being. Often those Netflix nights are a necessity; everyone's social battery is different, and moreover, no one should feel obligated to put themselves in situations where they don't feel respected or safe. Plus, learning to set healthy boundaries can be especially crucial for people who are neurodivergent. But healthy, intentional compartmentalizing is not the issue I'm talking about here. We have reached peak boundary setting while we are also the most isolated we've ever been (and not just the sad rich people we talked about earlier), in a loneliness epidemic that has only been further augmented by a literal pandemic.

According to research published in the journal *American Psychologist*, data collected across thirty-four different studies involving more than 200,000 participants found "a small but significant increase in loneliness during the pandemic—about a 5% increase in the prevalence of loneliness across the individual studies, on average."

Not to sound dramatic, but loneliness is a life-and-death issue. Social connections are *vital* to your long-term health, and if you don't start investing in them when you're younger, they unfortunately become more and more difficult to cultivate—especially if we as a society get set in self-isolating ways. A report from the National Academies of Sciences, Engineering, and Medicine (NASEM) found that "more than one-third of adults aged 45 and older feel lonely, and nearly one-fourth of adults aged 65 and older are considered to be socially isolated." It also found strong evidence that increased loneliness and social isolation significantly increase a person's risk of premature death from all causes. And marginalized groups, particularly members of the LGBTQ+ community and immigrants, appear to be most vulnerable to loneliness.

Loneliness is a systemic issue as much as it is an individual one—but unfortunately, just as with your money, no one is going to be able to fix any feelings of loneliness for you.

And through the process of writing this book, I started to notice a pattern: Nearly every single person I spoke with emphasized the importance of community. We tend to think of relationships as just one compartment of our lives, when in actuality they are woven into every facet. A fulfilling home life is founded on solid relationships, with either your partner, your family, or yourself. Your professional life is buoyed when you have the support of colleagues and a manager who advocates in your favor. And demystifying the process of earning more and wealth-building is a lot easier when you have people with whom you can talk about money openly.

Where Do You Draw the Line?

So that just lands you with another contradiction, right? *Set boundaries to protect your mental health, but don't go so hard that you self-care yourself into living the rest of your life in total isolation.* For Maria, it's important to remember that boundaries exist on a spectrum from loose to rigid. Too loose, and you run the risk of being taken advantage of, spending your time and money on things and activities that don't even really interest you, and not taking care of yourself. Too rigid, and you risk isolating yourself from the meaningful connections that are vital to your well-being. But in her opinion, to combat that rigidness, you have to think of fostering your social life as an ongoing practice, and you have to be flexible with it. "We think that if something is not a 'hell yes,' then it's definitely a 'hell no,'" she said. "But sometimes it's a 'Hmm, I'm not completely sold on this, but maybe I should go,' and then you end up having a really great time. . . . We know that, in terms of mental health, isolation is probably one of the worst things that we can do for ourselves, but it's also really comfortable and cozy to be at home alone."

Of course, thinking in terms of a "practice" can make socializing and cultivating community feel like a chore—and unfortunately, it might feel that way at first. "I don't want to equate it to this idea of going to the gym," said Maria, "but you *have* to make an extra effort. And after you're done with the gym, you're just like, 'Oh my gosh, that was amazing, I feel so great, I feel energized.' Relationships are kind of like that. They take effort. They don't just fall into your lap."

But like everything else, it's about striking the right balance. "If you're constantly staying at home and that's your self-care, and you're not interacting with anybody, then you need to figure something else out for yourself," Maria said. "But if you're constantly saying yes to everything and you're overextending, then maybe you'd be better off taking some time to yourself and resting." Sure, you have to learn to say no in order to make yes more meaningful—but the opposite is true, too.

I don't want to pretend it's easy or straightforward to start saying yes first, or at least more, especially if you're in the middle of a particularly busy or stressful time. But loneliness and isolation can often compound. New parents, for instance, are faced with a completely life-changing period that basically requires upheaving their typical routines, which can cause loneliness to feel extreme. According to a study by the British Red Cross, "More than eight in 10 mothers (83%) under the age of 30 had feelings of loneliness some of the time, while 43% said they felt lonely all the time." Sometimes being more isolated is a fact of life (*gestures to the general shitshow that started in 2020*). So when you're in a lonelier phase, you have to remember what Eve Rodsky had to say about taking an interest in your own life: It's not optional. Even if you can't possibly make time for your friends and loved ones right now, you have to figure out a way to ease back into it and not let yourself default to self-isolating.

If you feel overwhelmingly lonely, know that it's not your fault. We live in a particular era of capitalism that rewards isolation, from same-day deliveries that mean we never have to visit a brick-and-mortar store again to virtual alternatives to every possible real-life social opportunity, from workout classes to happy hours. And, of course, especially for those of us in our twenties and thirties, we often equate socializing with having to "go out"—a beloved pastime for some, but a real source of anxiety and dread for others. There's value in the occasional night spent letting loose with friends, but it's not at all a requirement for maintaining and building relationships if that's not your vibe. Here are some rules that I've found helpful when it comes to investing in your long-term social wellness:

- Before you automatically say no, ask yourself, *Am I saying no because I genuinely don't want to do this thing? Am I saying no because I've been overextending myself and know that I'll need a break? Or am I saying no because it's slightly inconvenient?*

- Budget your social time the way you do your money—and actually spend your allotted budget. That means making it a goal to socialize (outside of a romantic relationship) at least once a week, if not more frequently.

- Remember that no one person should be responsible for your entire social well-being. Not your husband, not your best friend, not your child. That doesn't mean you need to go out and make a million acquaintances if you tend to lean toward introversion, but we need all kinds of relationships in our lives in order to feel fulfilled.

- Having a healthy social life doesn't mean always hanging out in a group setting. Some of us feel much more fulfilled having one-on-one time with a friend or loved one, and that totally counts.

- If it doesn't come naturally to you, you do not have to magically become spontaneous in order to maintain your social health. Scheduling time to hang out doesn't make you an unfun nuisance; it makes you considerate.

- A boundary is still a boundary even if it's flexible. If a friend asks you to do something that's out of your budget or simply doesn't sound worth spending money on to you, there is no shame in offering an alternative.

Don't automatically turn down opportunities for new experiences, but do know your limits.

Inconvenience: The Answer to Putting Yourself First

It doesn't matter if we're discussing your social well-being, unlearning the habits that have led you to burnout, reexamining your wealth-building strategy, or interrogating how you show up in the workplace. The message I most want to leave you with is this:

No matter what the question is, the answer is often to choose the less convenient option.

Boundaries are not meant to help you shut yourself off from the possibility of a full and wonderful life. The entire point of setting boundaries is to clarify what matters to you so that you can stop letting what doesn't matter cloud your judgment and take up your energy. Self-care is not about finding quick fixes, but about making decisions based on what's actually best for you. Sometimes you must think of your future self instead of what's easiest right now. And this applies to everything I've put in this book.

It is easier, in the short term, to stick to the status quo in your home life. But will that allow you to feel seen, respected, and like you're contributing to an equitable home life in the long run?

It is tempting to throw out all your financial goals in favor of impulsive decisions that make you momentarily feel free. But are those moments worth the security and legitimate freedom you could give yourself in the long run?

It is comfortable never to speak up at work, assert your own boundaries, or advocate for anyone else's. But will it have been worth it if things don't change? Isn't that a scarier thought than the possibility that they *could*?

It's devastating to realize you can't budget or life-hack your way out of a difficult financial or emotional situation. There are always going to be people with more—people with too much—who can easily bypass the "character building" moments of struggle most of us have to endure in order to get anywhere worthwhile. There are so many systemic issues that need to be changed so that all of us can live with the security and fulfillment we deserve. But these realities are not reasons to give in to useless nihilism and not even try, especially when useful nihilism is right there, asking you, *Why not try?* Defaulting to convenience is a short-term recipe for long-term resentment. You don't want to regret not learning to put yourself first.

Don't aim for the most money or the healthiest appearance or the most prestigious job title or the biggest home or the earliest retirement. "Most" and "best" are empty signifiers, because there will always be someone else who comes along to usurp that place. Simply aim for *enough*. Enough time to spend with your loved ones, even when you're resisting the pull of hustle culture. Enough energy to spend on the experiences that make you feel completely alive, even if it's something as mind-boggling as willingly jumping into an ice-cold ocean. Enough interest in your job that you feel useful and stimulated, even if you're comfortable leaving at 5:00 P.M. sharp every day. Enough self-awareness to know when it's time to walk away, even if it means giving up an impressive promotion or a substantial raise. Enough money to try to consistently live by your own values, even when there's so much beyond your control. And enough confidence to know that it doesn't matter how any of this looks to anyone else, as long as you're content with your own decisions.

You deserve to invest in everything: in your finances, in your relationships, in your mental health, in your workplace culture, in your own damn free time, in experiences that make you think, *I can't believe I just did that.* You deserve the contentment that comes with choosing, over and over again, the less convenient option. You don't deserve moments of joy: You deserve a lifetime of it.

FILL ME IN

Final Questions for Reflection

Now that you've worked through this whole book, let's revisit our self-guided questions from the beginning, tweaked to fit this holistic lens you should (hopefully) be able to give yourself and your life:

When looking at your life right now, what's working? What needs improvement?

How have you changed (or are planning to change) your day-to-day choices in order to fit the life you actually want?

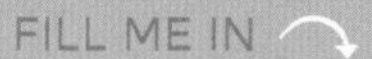

How are you working toward adding hours to your week? How are you spending them?

How are you redefining your roles in order to feel more in control of your time?

FILL ME IN

A year from now, how do you want to define yourself? What are you doing to work toward that? Use all of this space to brainstorm, make notes, and create a vision for yourself.

FILL ME IN

ACKNOWLEDGMENTS

All our thanks to Libby Burton for being the kindest, most perceptive editor and biggest champion of the book we were meant to publish, and to the entire team at Crown Currency for their belief that a book can be beautiful and still be important. To Anthony Mattero for his priceless insight and confidence in TFD's mission. To Lindsay Bryan-Podvin, Richard Coffin, Tiffany Dufu, Amanda Holden, Ryan Houlihan, Christina Mychas, Jazmine Reed, Eve Rodsky, Maria Sosa, and Cindy Zuniga-Sanchez, without whose wisdom this book would have been unimaginably harder to write. To Cindy Niu, whose incredible illustrations brought this book to life. To our parents, Jan and Will Trantham and Karen and Mark Ver Hage, whose faith in us has propelled us farther than we could have imagined. To Chelsea Fagan, our fearless leader, without whom this book and the thoughts inside it simply wouldn't exist. And to the entire TFD team—this book is as much yours as it is ours.

20 **"Ramsey Solutions provides"** "Dave's Story," Ramsey Solutions, accessed April 21, 2023, https://www.ramseysolutions.com/company/history/daves-story.

20 **debt snowball method** "Debt Snowball Calculator," Ramsey Solutions, accessed April 21, 2023, https://www.ramseysolutions.com/debt/debt-snowball-calculator.

21 **In 2021, a former employee** Maria Cramer, "Dave Ramsey Fired Employee for Taking Covid Precautions, Suit Says," *The New York Times*, Dec. 14, 2021, https://www.nytimes.com/2021/12/14/us/dave-ramsey-lawsuit-covid.html.

21 **The company settled a separate lawsuit** Liam Adams, "Ramsey Solutions Settles Discrimination Lawsuit from Former Employee Who Came Out as Lesbian," *The Tennessean*, June 30, 2022, https://www.tennessean.com/story/news/religion/2022/06/23/dave-ramseys-company-settles-lawsuit-alleging-lgbtq-discrimination/7697697001/.

21 **Evangelical belief system he belongs to** Kristen Bahler, "Broke Millennials Are Flocking to Financial Guru Dave Ramsey. Is His Advice Any Good?," *Money*, April 16, 2019, https://money.com/dave-ramsey-money-debt-free/.

21 **America was founded under** George Monbiot, "Puritanism of the Rich," *The Guardian*, Nov. 9, 2004, https://www.theguardian.com/world/2004/nov/09/usa.comment.

22 **"If you're working on paying"** Dave Ramsey, Twitter post, Feb. 7, 2020, https://twitter.com/DaveRamsey status/1229425772546449409?lang=mr.

22 **a 2017 study** Julie Zauzmer, "Christians Are More than Twice as Likely to Blame a Person's Poverty on Lack of Effort," *The Washington Post*, Aug. 3, 2017, https://www.washingtonpost.com/news/acts-of-faith/wp/2017/08/03/christians-are-more-than-twice-as-likely-to-blame-a-persons-poverty-on-lack-of-effort/.

23 **"women are more susceptible"** U. Orth, R. W. Robins, and C. J. Soto, "Tracking the Trajectory of Shame, Guilt, and Pride Across the

Life Span," *Journal of Personality and Social Psychology*, 99, no. 6 (2010): 1061–71, https://doi.org/10.1037/a0021342.

24 **intuitive eating** "10 Principles of Intuitive Eating," *Intuitive Eating*, Dec. 19, 2019, https://www.intuitiveeating.org/10-principles-of-intuitive-eating/.

28 **50/30/20 budget** Elizabeth Warren and Amelia Warren Tyagi, *All Your Worth: The Ultimate Lifetime Money Plan* (New York: Free Press, 2006).

31 **In 2007, Congress** "Congressman Cohen Reintroduces $15 Minimum Wage Bill," Congressman Steve Cohen website, Jan. 25, 2023, https://cohen.house.gov/media-center/press-releases/congressman-cohen-reintroduces-15-minimum-wage-bill.

38 **Almost half of Americans** Maurie Backman, "47% of Americans Can't Handle a $500 Emergency Without Worry," *The Motley Fool*, Feb. 4, 2022, https://www.fool.com/the-ascent/personal-finance/articles/47-of-americans-cant-handle-a-500-emergency-without-worry/.

39 **one now-famous study** Daniel Kahneman and Angus Deaton, "High Income Improves Evaluation of Life but Not Emotional Well-Being," *Proceedings of the National Academy of Sciences* 107, no. 38 (2010): 16489–93, https://doi.org/10.1073/pnas.1011492107.

39 **while others have claimed** Gabrielle Olya, "What Is the Minimum Salary You Need to Be Happy in Every State?," GOBankingRates, April 15, 2023, https://www.gobankingrates.com/money/wealth/minimum-salary-to-be-happy-state/.

40 **As part of the Harvard Study** Liz Mineo, "Genes Are Nice, but Joy Is Better," *Harvard Gazette*, April 11, 2017, https://news.harvard.edu/gazette/story/2017/04/over-nearly-80-years-harvard-study-has-been-showing-how-to-live-a-healthy-and-happy-life/.

40 **A different report** Karen Salmansohn, "The No. 1 Contributor to Happiness," *Psychology Today*, accessed April 23, 2023, https://www.psychologytoday.com/us/blog/bouncing-back/201106/the-no-1-contributor-happiness.

40 **"Knowing yourself involves knowing"** Zameena Mejia, "The Key to Your Happiness Depends on These 2 Things, According to Self-Help Expert Gretchen Rubin," CNBC, Nov. 3, 2017, https://www.cnbc.com/2017/11/03/gretchen-rubin-the-key-to-your-happiness-depends-on-these-2-things.html.

41 **In a 2016 study** Josh Rosenblat, "The Wealthier You Get, the Less Social You Are. Here's Why It Matters," *Vox*, May 5, 2016, https://www.vox.com/2016/5/5/11578994/income-friends-family.

41 **A 2014 study** Maia Szalavitz, "The Rich Are Different: More Money, Less Empathy," *Time*, Nov. 24, 2010, https://healthland.time.com/2010/11/24/the-rich-are-different-more-money-less-empathy/.

42 **Friendships last** Elizabeth DeVita-Raeburn, "Empathy: How It Changes Your Friendships, Job and Life," *Self*, Dec. 14, 2011, https://www.self.com/story/how-empathy-changes-friendships-jobs-life.

42 **"empathetic accuracy"** Szalavitz, "The Rich Are Different."

43 **"can [kick-start] the release"** Dr. Tian Dayton, "Money Addiction," *HuffPost*, Nov. 17, 2011, https://www.huffpost.com/entry/money-addiction_b_221937.

43 **the World Health Organization estimates** "Statistics on Process Addiction," The Recovery Village, June 3, 2022, https://www.therecoveryvillage.com/process-addiction/behavioral-addiction-statistics/.

44 **golden handcuffs** Will Kenton, "What Are Golden Handcuffs? Definition, Purpose, and Examples," *Investopedia*, June 29, 2021, https://www.investopedia.com/terms/g/goldenhandcuffs.asp.

49 **3.8% on average** "Inflation Rates in the United States of America," Worlddata.info, accessed April 23, 2023, https://www.worlddata.info/america/usa/inflation-rates.php.

49 **"Inflation" refers to** Ceyda Oner, "Inflation: Prices on the Rise," IMF, July 30, 2019, https://www.imf.org/en/Publications/fandd/issues/Series/Back-to-Basics/Inflation.

57 **Crypto Key Terms** Jake Frankenfield, "Cryptocurrency Explained with Pros and Cons for Investment," *Investopedia*, April 23, 2023, https://www.investopedia.com/terms/c/cryptocurrency.asp.

57 **because of the way the technology** "What Is Blockchain Technology?," *CB Insights Research*, Nov. 10, 2021, https://www.cbinsights.com/research/what-is-blockchain-technology/.

57 **the average investor is rarely good** Lyle Daly, "Is Stock Picking Worth It? Here's Why I Stopped Doing It," *The Motley Fool*, Nov. 22, 2022, https://www.fool.com/the-ascent/buying-stocks/articles/is-stock-picking-worth-it-heres-why-i-stopped-doing-it/.

58 **The greater fool theory** Ryan Browne, "Bill Gates Says Crypto and NFTs Are '100% Based on Greater Fool Theory,'" CNBC, June 15, 2022, https://www.cnbc.com/2022/06/15/bill-gates-says-crypto-and-nfts-are-based-on-greater-fool-theory.html.

59 **Paris Hilton** *The Tonight Show Starring Jimmy Fallon*, season 9, episode 73, Jan. 24, 2022.

59 **One of the most massive crypto** Jacquelyn Melinek, "Former FTX CEO SBF Pleads Not Guilty to US Criminal Charges," TechCrunch, Jan. 3, 2023, https://techcrunch.com/2023/01/03/ftx-former-ceo-sbf-pleads-not-guilty-to-u-s-criminal-charges/.

63 **the average stock market return** Andrew J. Dehan, "What Is the Average Stock Market Rate of Return?," *SmartAsset*, accessed March 17, 2023, https://smartasset.com/investing/stock-market-rate-of-return.

64 **financial independence** Miriam Caldwell, "What Does Financially Independent Mean?," *The Balance*, July 1, 2022, https://www.thebalancemoney.com/when-should-i-become-financially-independent-2385820.

65 **1 in 10 women** "Older Women and Poverty: Single and Minority Women," WISER, accessed April 21, 2023, https://wiserwomen.org/fact-sheets/facts-and-solutions/older-women-and-poverty-single-minority-women/.

70 **the 4% rule** Julia Kagan, "What Is the 4% Rule for Withdrawals in Retirement and How Much Can You Spend?" *Investopedia,* Jan. 20, 2022, https://www.investopedia.com/terms/f/four-percent-rule.asp.

71 **one provided by the U.S. government** "Compound Interest Calculator," Investor.gov, accessed April 21, 2023, https://www.investor.gov/financial-tools-calculators/calculators/compound-interest-calculator.

76 **top 5%** Emily A. Shrider et al., "Income and Poverty in the United States: 2020," Census.gov, accessed June 9, 2022, https://www.census.gov/library/publications/2021/demo/p60-273.html.

77 **"availability of federal funding"** "Fact Sheet: President Biden Announces Student Loan Relief for Borrowers Who Need It Most," The White House, Aug. 24, 2022, https://www.whitehouse.gov/briefing-room/statements-releases/2022/08/24/fact-sheet-president-biden-announces-student-loan-relief-for-borrowers-who-need-it-most/.

78 **"Opinion: Biden's student loan"** Charlie Dent, "Opinion: Biden's Student Loan Forgiveness Is Unfair and Unwise," CNN, Aug. 26, 2022, https://www.cnn.com/2022/08/26/opinions/biden-student-loan-forgiveness-unfair-dent/index.html.

78 **"Student loan 'forgiveness'"** "Student Loan 'Forgiveness' Is a Liberal Sacrifice to Millennial Resentments," AMAC Newsline, American Association of Mature American Citizens, Aug. 30, 2022, https://amac.us/student-loan-forgiveness-is-a-liberal-sacrifice-to-millennial-resentments/.

79 **when adjusted for inflation** "Real and Nominal Value of the Minimum Wage U.S. 2022," Statista, accessed Jan. 30, 2023, https://www.statista.com/statistics/1065466/real-nominal-value-minimum-wage-us/.

79 **And again adjusting** Melanie Hanson, "College Tuition Inflation [2023]: Rate Increase Statistics," Education Data Initiative, Aug. 10, 2022, https://educationdata.org/college-tuition-inflation-rate.

79 **In her book** Anne Helen Petersen, "Our Burnt-Out Parents," essay in *Can't Even: How Millennials Became the Burnout Generation* (Boston: Mariner Books, 2020).

80 **The G.I. Bill** "How the GI Bill's Promise Was Denied to a Million Black WWII Veterans," History.com, accessed April 23, 2023, https://www.history.com/news/gi-bill-black-wwii-veterans-benefits.

80 **Black borrowers have been hit** "Fact Sheet: President Biden Announces Student Loan Relief."

80 **"Black women are paid"** "Deeper in Debt: Women and Student Loans," AAUW, Aug. 26, 2021, https://www.aauw.org/resources/research/deeper-in-debt/.

80 **"women from marginalized communities"** Victoria Jackson and Brittani Williams, "How Black Women Experience Student Debt," The Education Trust, accessed Feb. 22, 2023, https://edtrust.org/resource/how-black-women-experience-student-debt.

93 **as of April 2022** "Shein: The Unacceptable Face of Throwaway Fast Fashion," *The Guardian,* April 10, 2022, https://www.theguardian.com/fashion/2022/apr/10/shein-the-unacceptable-face-of-throwaway-fast-fashion.

93 **Shein only needs a week** DW Planet A, "If You Think Fast Fashion Is Bad, Check Out SHEIN," YouTube, Dec. 10, 2021, https://www.youtube.com/watch?v=U4km0Cslcpg.

93 **"real-time retail"** Packy McCormick, "Shein: The TikTok of Ecommerce," *Not Boring by Packy McCormick,* May 17, 2021, https://www.notboring.co/p/shein-the-tiktok-of-ecommerce?s=r.

93 **Swiss watchdog Public Eye** Chavie Lieber, "Report: Shein Violating Labour Laws," The Business of Fashion, Nov. 19, 2021, https://www.businessoffashion.com/news/retail/report-shein-violating-labour-laws/.

93 **A separate investigation** Sangeeta Singh-Kurtz, "Shein Is Even Worse Than You Thought," The Cut, Oct. 17, 2022, https://www.thecut.com/2022/10/shein-is-treating-workers-even-worse-than-you-thought.html.

93 **the fast-fashion industry is responsible** Marthe de Ferrer, "How Are Shein Hauls Making Our Planet Unlivable?" Euronews, Oct. 17, 2022,

https://www.euronews.com/green/2022/10/17/how-are-shein-hauls-making-our-planet-unlivable.

96 **Tony Robbins** "What Is an Abundance Mindset?," tonyrobbins.com, Dec. 4, 2021, https://www.tonyrobbins.com/mind-meaning/adopt-abundance-mindset/.

96 **Rachel Hollis** "Rachel Hollis: Manifest Success, and Manage Negative Feedback," *The School of Greatness* podcast, Aug. 12, 2022, https://lewishowes.com/podcast/rachel-hollis-manifest-success-overcome-guilt-manage-negative-feedback/.

102 **the S&P 500** Katie Brockman, "Worried About the Stock Market? 3 Must-See Statistics to Calm Your Nerves," Nasdaq, accessed April 23, 2023, https://www.nasdaq.com/articles/worried-about-the-stock-market-3-must-see-statistics-to-calm-your-nerves.

103 **published on CNBC** Zack Guzman, "This Simple Tipping Trick Could Save You over $400 a Year," CNBC, April 9, 2019, https://www.cnbc.com/2018/02/12/tipping-trick-could-save-you-over-400-a-year.html.

104 **The federal minimum wage** Alison Doyle, "Minimum Wage for Employees Who Receive Tips," The Balance, Jan. 2, 2023, https://www.thebalancemoney.com/minimum-wage-for-workers-who-receive-tips-2062119.

118 **Visualization is a tool** "Seeing Is Believing: The Power of Visualization," *Psychology Today*, accessed April 23, 2023, https://www.psychologytoday.com/us/blog/flourish/200912/seeing-is-believing-the-power-visualization.

118 **publicizing her transcendental meditation practice** Claire Hoffman, "David Lynch Is Back . . . as a Guru of Transcendental Meditation," *The New York Times Magazine*, Feb. 24, 2013, http://www.nytimes.com/2013/02/24/magazine/david-lynch-transcendental-meditation.html.

119 **Someone doing the Lord's work** Nikhil Sonnad, "All the 'Wellness' Products Americans Love to Buy Are Sold on Both Infowars and Goop," *Quartz*, July 20, 2022, https://qz.com/1010684/all-the-wellness-products-american-love-to-buy-are-sold-on-both-infowars-and-goop.

119 **Goop even landed itself** Sara Gaynes Levy, "Goop's Vaginal Jade Egg Just Sparked a $145,000 Lawsuit Settlement," *Vogue*, Sept. 5, 2018, https://www.vogue.com/article/goop-jade-yoni-egg-lawsuit-gwyneth-paltrow-vaginal-pelvic-floor-health.

119 **Gwyneth is under fire** "Gwyneth Paltrow x Dr. Will Cole: Intuitive Eating, Intermittent Fasting, Inflammation + The Future of Functional Medicine," in The Art of Being Well with Dr. Will Cole, podcast, Apple Podcasts, Feb. 25, 2021, https://podcasts.apple.com/us/podcast/gwyneth-paltrow-x-dr-will-cole-intuitive-eating-intermittent/id1539535133?i=1000510587596.

119 **functional medicine expert** "About Dr. Will Cole," Dr. Will Cole website, accessed Feb. 21, 2023, https://drwillcole.com/about.

119 **a practice that is not** Amber Middleton, "Gwyneth Paltrow Says Rectal Ozone Therapy Was 'Very Helpful.' The FDA Says It Has No Medical Use," *Insider*, March 24, 2023, https://www.insider.com/gwyneth-paltrow-interview-what-rectal-ozone-therapy-goop-2023-3.

119 **a chemical most of us** Annette McDermott, "What Is Phosphatidylcholine and How Is It Used?," Healthline, Sept. 18, 2018, https://www.healthline.com/health/food-nutrition/phosphatidylcholine.

119 **a controversial diet regimen** "'Detoxes' and 'Cleanses': What You Need to Know," NCCIH, n.d., https://www.nccih.nih.gov/health/detoxes-and-cleanses-what-you-need-to-know.

119 **Goop also currently sells** "Goop Wellness G.Tox 7-Day Reset Kit," Goop, n.d., https://goop.com/goop-wellness-g-tox-7-day-reset-kit/p/?variant_id=95118.

119 **annual "wellness" weekend retreats** "IGH Los Angeles Pre-Sale Tickets Available," Goop, March 27, 2019, https://goop.com/igh-pre-sale-tickets/.

124 **In debt payoff** Ashley Eneriz, "Debt Avalanche vs. Debt Snowball: What's the Difference?," *Investopedia*, April 13, 2022, https://www.investopedia.com/articles/personal-finance/080716/debt-avalanche-vs-debt-snowball-which-best-you.asp.

134 **Imposter syndrome has been** Pauline Rose Clance and Suzanne Ament Imes, "The Imposter Phenomenon in High Achieving Women: Dynamics and Therapeutic Intervention," *Psychotherapy* 15, no. 3 (Jan. 1, 1978): 241–47, https://doi.org/10.1037/h0086006.

135 **a study conducted** "KPMG Study Finds 75% of Female Executives Across Industries Have Experienced Imposter Syndrome in Their Careers," Oct. 27, 2020, https://info.kpmg.us/news-perspectives/people-culture/kpmg-study-finds-most-female-executives-experience-imposter-syndrome.html.

135 **Market research technology firm** Brittany Nicols, "Are You an Imposter?," The InnovateMR Blog, n.d., https://blog.innovatemr.com/are-you-an-imposter?utm_source=PR_Newswire&utm_medium=Press_Release&utm_campaign=Release_2021.

135 **A report from LeanIn.org** "The State of Black Women in Corporate America," leanin.org, n.d., https://leanin.org/research/state-of-black-women-in-corporate-america/section-3-everyday-discrimination#.

137 **that meme of the two guys** "Two Guys on a Bus," Know Your Meme, April 12, 2023, https://knowyourmeme.com/memes/two-guys-on-a-bus.

139 **According to the advocacy group** Opportunity@Work, "The Paper Ceiling—Opportunity@work.org," June 6, 2022, https://opportunityatwork.org/thepaperceiling/.

139 **college enrollment dropped** Gitanjali Poonia, "College Enrollment Numbers Drop to Historic Lows," *Deseret News,* Jan. 13, 2022, https://www.deseret.com/2022/1/13/22882277/college-enrollment-numbers-drop-to-historic-lows.

139 **A 2021 Insight Center report** Kwame Anthony Appiah, "The Myth of Meritocracy: Who Really Gets What They Deserve?," *The Guardian,* Oct. 19, 2018, https://www.theguardian.com/news/2018/oct/19/the-myth-of-meritocracy-who-really-gets-what-they-deserve.

146 **National Labor Relations Act** "Your Right to Discuss Wages," National Labor Relations Board, n.d., https://www.nlrb.gov/about-nlrb/rights-we-protect/your-rights/your-rights-to-discuss-wages.

146 **You can find out** "Jurisdictional Standards," National Labor Relations Board, n.d., https://www.nlrb.gov/about-nlrb/rights-we-protect/the-law/jurisdictional-standards.

151 **For tipped service workers** "Minimum Wages for Tipped Employees," U.S. Department of Labor, n.d., https://www.dol.gov/agencies/whd/state/minimum-wage/tipped.

152 **Companies like Chipotle** Miranda Marquit, "12 Companies That Will Pay for Your College Education," *Investopedia,* Nov. 29, 2022, https://www.investopedia.com/companies-pay-college-6829220.

156 **sitcom trope** "Foolish Husband, Responsible Wife," TV Tropes, n.d., https://tvtropes.org/pmwiki/pmwiki.php/Main/FoolishHusbandResponsibleWife.

156 **American women have largely** "Civilian Labor Force by Sex," U.S. Department of Labor, n.d., https://www.dol.gov/agencies/wb/data/lfp/civilianlfbysex.

157 **According to a 2018 article** Claire Cain Miller, "How Same-Sex Couples Divide Chores, and What It Reveals About Modern Parenting," *The New York Times,* May 16, 2018, https://www.nytimes.com/2018/05/16/upshot/same-sex-couples-divide-chores-much-more-evenly-until-they-become-parents.html.

158 **Here's an excerpt** Jennifer Szalai, "The Complicated Origins of 'Having It All,'" *The New York Times Magazine,* Jan. 2, 2015, https://www.nytimes.com/2015/01/04/magazine/the-complicated-origins-of-having-it-all.html.

160 **Researchers have found** Michael Bittman, Paula England, Liana Sayer, Nancy Folbre, and George Matheson, "When Does Gender Trump Money? Bargaining and Time in Household Work," *American Journal of Sociology* 109, no. 1 (July 1, 2003): 186–214, https://doi.org/10.1086/378341.

161 **In 2017** Claire Howorth, "Motherhood Is Hard to Get Wrong. So Why Do So Many Moms Feel So Bad About Themselves?," *Time,* Oct. 19, 2017, https://time.com/4989068/motherhood-is-hard-to-get-wrong/.

162 **According to the study** "Research Shows Moms with Husbands or Live-In Male Partners Do More Housework Than Single Moms," Population Reference Bureau, n.d., https://www.prb.org/news/mothers-day/.

167 **family and consumer science** Tove Danovich, "Despite a Revamped Focus on Real-Life Skills, 'Home Ec' Classes Fade Away," NPR, June 14, 2018, https://www.npr.org/sections/thesalt/2018/06/14/618329461/despite-a-revamped-focus-on-real-life-skills-home-ec-classes-fade-away.

167 **"According to Oxfam"** Angela Garbes, "The Devaluation of Care Work Is by Design," *The Atlantic,* May 13, 2022, https://www.theatlantic.com/family/archive/2022/05/unpaid-domestic-labor-essential-work/629839/.

174 **According to a KPMG study** "KPMG Study Finds 75% of Female Executives Across Industries Have Experienced Imposter Syndrome in Their Careers," KPMG.

175 **"I have the best advice"** *Variety,* "Kim Kardashian's Business Advice: 'Get Your F**king Ass Up and Work,'" YouTube video, March 9, 2022, https://www.youtube.com/watch?v=XX2izzshRmI.

176 **"As an assistant editor"** Jessica DeFino, "I Worked My Ass Off for the Kardashian-Jenner Apps. I Couldn't Afford Gas," *Vice,* April 12, 2022, https://www.vice.com/en/article/bvnky4/i-worked-my-ass-off-for-kim-kardashian-jenner-apps-i-couldnt-afford-gas-jessica-defino.

176 ***Forbes* initially doubled down** Kerry A. Dolan, "Here's What Forbes Means by Self-Made: From Bootstrappers to Silver Spooners," *Forbes,* July 13, 2018, https://www.forbes.com/sites/kerryadolan/2018/07/13/heres-what-forbes-means-by-self-made-from-bootstrappers-to-silver-spooners/#267b19541ca3.

176 **as of this writing** "Instagram Accounts with the Most Followers Worldwide as of July 2023," Statista, Jan. 24, 2023, https://www.statista.com/statistics/421169/most-followers-instagram/.

176 **maintains that she inherited nothing** Katherine Gillespie, "Kylie Jenner: Get Rich or Die Following," *PAPER Magazine,* Feb 19, 2019,

https://www.papermag.com/kylie-jenner-transformation-2629088275.html#rebelltitem8.

177 **it was revealed** Chase Peterson-Withorn, "Inside Kylie Jenner's Web of Lies—and Why She's No Longer a Billionaire," *Forbes*, May 29, 2020, https://www.forbes.com/sites/chasewithorn/2020/05/29/inside-kylie-jennerss-web-of-lies-and-why-shes-no-longer-a-billionaire/?sh=7ffb54eb25f7.

177 **excluding the nose jobs** Lorry Hill, "Kim Kardashian: Plastic Surgery (2000–2020) | FACE Edition," YouTube video, Aug. 23, 2020, https://www.youtube.com/watch?v=X6AbCty25H0.

177 **selling a "micro bikini"** Leyla Mohammed, "Kim Kardashian's Skims Bikini Compared to Size of Tortilla Chips on TikTok," *BuzzFeed News*, Feb. 8, 2023, https://www.buzzfeednews.com/article/leylamohammed/kim-kardashian-skims-bikini-size-tortilla-chips-viral-tiktok.

178 **Both Kim Kardashian's** Solene Rauturier, "How Ethical Is Good American?," Good On You, Feb. 8, 2023, https://goodonyou.eco/how-ethical-is-good-american/.

178 **everything from crypto** Matt Binder, "Kim Kardashian Fined $1.26 Million by the SEC for Promoting Cryptocurrency on Instagram," Mashable, Oct. 3, 2022, https://mashable.com/article/kim-kardashian-sec-fine-cryptocurrency.

178 **"detoxifying" teas and shakes** Gabby Landsverk, "Khloe Kardashian Promoted Flat Tummy Shakes Again, and Influencers Are Warning They Promote Risky Dieting Habits," *Insider*, Jan. 10, 2020, https://www.insider.com/khloe-kardashian-vogue-williams-flat-belly-shakes-instagram-controversy-2020-1.

180 **2019 data from job board** "To Intern or Not to Intern: Which Companies Require an Internship?," Chegg Internships, Dec. 19, 2019, https://www.internships.com/career-advice/search/to-intern-or-not-which-companies-require-an-internship.

181 **According to the National Association** Michael J. Gaynor, "43 Percent of Internships at For-Profit Companies Don't Pay. This Man Is Helping to Change That," *Washington Post*, Jan. 15, 2019, https://www

.washingtonpost.com/lifestyle/magazine/his-quest-to-get-interns-paid-is-paying-off/2019/01/11/93df2b2a-ff2a-11e8-83c0-b06139e540e5_story.html.

182 **According to the 2022 Women** McKinsey & Company, "Women in the Workplace 2022," McKinsey & Company, Oct. 17, 2022, https://www.mckinsey.com/featured-insights/diversity-and-inclusion/women-in-the-workplace.

183 **According to a study from project** Tracy Brower, PhD, "Burnout Is a Worldwide Problem: 5 Ways Work Must Change," *Forbes*, July 24, 2022, https://www.forbes.com/sites/tracybrower/2022/07/24/burnout-is-a-worldwide-problem-5-ways-work-must-change/.

183 **According to data from job** Kim Elsesser, "Women of Color Set Lower Salary Requirements Than White Men, According to Job Search Site," *Forbes*, Feb. 6, 2023, https://www.forbes.com/sites/kimelsesser/2023/02/06/women-of-color-set-lower-salary-requirements-than-white-men-according-to-job-search-site/.

183 **with an increase of over 200,000** "Unionization Increased by 200,000 in 2022: Tens of Millions More Wanted to Join a Union, but Couldn't," Economic Policy Institute, Jan. 19, 2023, https://www.epi.org/publication/unionization-2022/.

196 **In 2022, 55% of PTO** Opheli Garcia Lawler, "Unused PTO Has Doubled Since 2019, Even as More Companies Offer It," *Thrillist*, Dec. 15, 2022, https://www.thrillist.com/news/nation/paid-time-off-vacation-days-unused-study.

197 **in an article for *Vice*** Shayla Love, "The Cult of Busyness," *Vice*, June 7, 2021, https://www.vice.com/en/article/k78wpz/covid-changed-our-relationship-to-busyness-can-we-keep-it-that-way-v28n2.

199 **"quiet quitting" has been covered** Alyson Krueger, "What Is Quiet Quitting and Who Is It For?," *The New York Times*, Aug. 24, 2022, https://www.nytimes.com/2022/08/23/style/quiet-quitting-tiktok.html.

199 **An article in *The Atlantic*** Derek Thompson, "Quiet Quitting Is a Fake Trend," *The Atlantic*, Sept. 16, 2022, https://www.theatlantic.com

/newsletters/archive/2022/09/quiet-quitting-trend-employee-disengagement/671436/.

199 **A 2022 Gallup poll** Jim Harter, "Is Quiet Quitting Real?," Gallup, April 18, 2023, https://www.gallup.com/workplace/398306/quiet-quitting-real.aspx.

214 **some even predicting** Larry Elliott, "Economics: Whatever Happened to Keynes' 15-Hour Working Week?," *The Guardian,* Aug. 31, 2008, https://www.theguardian.com/business/2008/sep/01/economics.

214 **the shareholder value-driven model** "The Productivity–Pay Gap," Economic Policy Institute, October 2022, https://www.epi.org/productivity-pay-gap/.

215 **the capital-owning class** Aimee Picchi, "The New Gilded Age: 2,750 People Have More Wealth Than Half the Planet," CBS News, Dec. 7, 2021, https://www.cbsnews.com/news/wealth-inequality-billionaires-piketty-report/.

216 **The data that shows that the wealthy** David Chang, "How Many Hours Do Rich People Work? You May Be Surprised," *The Motley Fool,* Oct. 17, 2022, https://www.fool.com/the-ascent/personal-finance/articles/how-many-hours-do-rich-people-work-you-may-be-surprised/.

216 **a few heartening examples** "Amazon Labor Union," Amazon Labor Union, n.d., https://www.amazonlaborunion.org/.

217 **The four-day workweek had been** Joe Hernandez, "Dozens of U.K. Companies Will Keep the 4-Day Workweek After a Pilot Program Ends," NPR, Feb. 21, 2023, https://www.npr.org/2023/02/21/1158507132/uk-study-companies-four-day-workweek.

221 **In most white-collar jobs** Abby McCain, "25+ Wasting Time at Work Statistics [2023]: How Much Time Is Wasted at Work," Zippia, Dec. 15, 2022, https://www.zippia.com/advice/wasting-time-at-work-statistics/.

228 **"Capitalism has cornered us"** Tricia Hersey, *Rest Is Resistance: Free Yourself from Grind Culture and Reclaim Your Life* (London: Hachette UK, 2022).

228 **In a survey of 1,000** Jamie Ballard, "Women Are More Likely Than Men to Say They're a People-Pleaser, and Many Dislike Being Seen as One," YouGov, Aug. 22, 2022, https://today.yougov.com/topics/society/articles-reports/2022/08/22/women-more-likely-men-people-pleasing-poll.

228 **The message "protect your peace"** Robin D. Stone, "Protect Your Peace," *Psychology Today,* July 15, 2021, https://www.psychologytoday.com/us/blog/the-color-wellness/202107/protect-your-peace.

228 **including many queer and trans** Melanie Whyte, "How to Protect Your Mental Health as Anti-Gay Slurs Increase," *PopSugar,* Aug. 30, 2022, https://www.popsugar.com/love/anti-gay-slurs-increase-mental-health-tips-48930428.

229 **JOMO, the joy of missing out** Kristen Fuller, "JOMO: The Joy of Missing Out," *Psychology Today,* July 26, 2018, https://www.psychologytoday.com/us/blog/happiness-is-state-mind/201807/jomo-the-joy-missing-out.

230 **According to research published** "COVID-19 Pandemic Led to Increase in Loneliness Around the World," May 9, 2022, American Psychological Association, https://www.apa.org/news/press/releases/2022/05/covid-19-increase-loneliness.

230 **marginalized groups, particularly members** "Loneliness and Social Isolation Linked to Serious Health Conditions," CDC, n.d., https://www.cdc.gov/aging/publications/features/lonely-older-adults.html.

232 **"More than eight in 10 mothers"** Rhiannon Lucy Cosslett, "Loneliness Is a Struggle for New Parents—Can We All Stop Pretending Everything's OK?," *The Guardian,* Oct. 25, 2022, https://www.theguardian.com/commentisfree/2022/oct/25/loneliness-new-parents-cuts-services-isolation.

INDEX

ABOUT THE AUTHORS

Holly Trantham has been with the TFD team since September 2016, working her way up from managing editor to creative director. In her free time, you can almost always find her devouring a romance novel or a slice of cake (or both simultaneously). She lives in Brooklyn with her husband and two tuxedo cats.

Lauren Ver Hage is The Financial Diet's co-founder and chief design officer. She oversees all of TFD's branding and design across print, social, video, and events. She also designed TFD's first book, *The Financial Diet: A Total Beginner's Guide to Getting Good with Money*. She lives in New Jersey with her husband, daughter, and dog.

Chelsea Fagan is a writer, a home cook, and the co-founder and CEO of The Financial Diet. She lives in Manhattan with her husband and dog.